STORIES OF King David

by Lillian S. Freehof

ILLUSTRATED by Seymour R. Kaplan

PHILADELPHIA
THE JEWISH PUBLICATION SOCIETY OF AMERICA

Copyright, 1952, by

THE JEWISH PUBLICATION SOCIETY OF AMERICA

Second Impression, 1956

MANUFACTURED IN THE UNITED STATES OF AMERICA BY
BOOK CRAFTSMEN ASSOCIATES, INC., NEW YORK

*Dedicated
With Love
to
My Brothers
and
My Sisters*

Acknowledgments

It is the nature of folklore to be written and rewritten by many authors in many centuries. Each author of such stories should be grateful to all the generations that precede him. I am thankful, first of all, for that spirit of playful learning which preserved and transmitted the lighter part of talmudic and midrashic literature; but I am specifically grateful to Dr. Louis Ginzberg who, in his monumental work, "The Legends of the Jews," and in his inexhaustible Notes to that work, has provided a rich treasure for all students in the field.

To Dr. Solomon Grayzel I should like to express my gratitude for his encouragement and patient help in preparing this manuscript for publication.

To Mr. Seymour R. Kaplan I extend my profound thanks for the vivid and charming fashion in which he illustrated the stories.

And to my dear husband, Dr. Solomon B. Freehof, who awakened my interest in the rich world of talmudic and midrashic thought and who encouraged me with his constant guidance, goes my especial gratitude.

L. S. F.

Contents

1. The Gift of Years
2. The Mystery of the Honey Jars
3. The Stubborn Oil
4. The King's Armor
5. The Five Pebbles
6. David and the Spider
7. The Madman of Gath
8. Abner and the Wasp
9. The Crumbling Walls
10. Footsteps in the Branches
11. The Giant Slingshot
12. Sixty Breaths of Sleep
13. Between Sky and Earth
14. The Key Which Unlocked the Rain
15. The Tumbling Priests
16. The Talking Shard
17. House of David
18. The Frog's Rebuke
19. The Magic Crown
20. The Guard of Eagles
21. The Pasha's Dagger

The Gift of Years

On the sixth day of Creation, two Archangels sat beside the Throne of Glory. Michael, the Prince of Wisdom, sat on the right hand. On the left sat Gabriel, the Prince of Strength. They were speaking of how the Lord had created the world.

He had formed the earth out of chaos. Day had been separated from night. The sun and the moon and the stars had been set on their course in the heavens. And on the earth, the beasts of the field, the birds of the air and the fish of the sea had been assigned to their dwelling-places.

Then Gabriel said, "Now, O Lord, Your world is complete. You have the angels and the elements, the earth and the sun, the moon and the sea. It is now sufficient."

But Michael smiled. "You know well, Gabriel, that God's world could not be complete until He had created man. I recall how the angels did object, saying, 'What is man that Thou art mindful of him?' Now man *does* exist. He now lives on earth."

"Aye," said the Lord. "This day have I created man. Now look you down into My Garden of Eden. See My child, the man Adam."

Gabriel and Michael looked through the golden clouds and the silvery clouds, then through the cobweby clouds that the earth sees. Their eyes pierced the mist and they saw into the Garden.

The whole of the Garden of Eden lay revealed under their gaze. They saw all four gardens divided by the four rivers flowing to the four corners of the earth refreshed by the four winds to bring the four seasons of the year.

In the Garden, at the center of the river that went out of Eden, were clear pools of water and splashing fountains. There, under a plum tree sat Adam, the most beautiful of God's creations.

"I see him, O Lord," Gabriel said. "I see in the Garden this noble creature You have fashioned. How long will he endure? This man Adam, how long will his breath last? How long will he live?"

"Not as long as you, My angels," God said. "You have existed with Me before Creation. You will continue with Me through all eternity. But man's life will be brief."

"How brief?" Gabriel asked. "How long will he live?"

"A long time to him," God answered. "Though it might seem brief to us. To My son Adam have I granted the privilege of living one of the heavenly days."

"Then he will live a thousand years on earth?" Gabriel asked.

"One thousand earthly years are Adam's. That does not seem so much, but Adam will be satisfied, for most of the children of men will live but threescore years and ten."

Michael nodded. "Seventy earth years."

"But some men will not be satisfied," Gabriel objected.

"That's why no man should know how much life he will have," Michael said. "Life is a precious thing. Every man will want as much of it as possible. If a man knows he is to have only forty years and he wants eighty, he will be disappointed. He will spend his forty years in grumbling and in bitterness. He will waste those forty years yearning for what he cannot have."

Gabriel agreed. "Aye. I see that. Then it is better for a man never to know how long he will live."

"That is My plan," said God. "No man shall ever know the length of his days. Except Adam, the first man. It is My wish that Adam should know that he is to have one thousand earth years of life. Go then, My angels, go down to the Garden of Eden and take that message to My son Adam."

Down on earth, in the Garden of Eden, Adam was still marvelling over everything he saw. He had just awakened to life and was filled with the wonder of it. The air was fragrant with the perfume of flowers and throughout the Garden were many, many trees.

All of life was still so new to Adam that every flower seemed the most perfect thing he had seen until he saw the grass, and then every blade of grass was the most beautiful thing he had seen until he saw the sun.

He was so enchanted with the wonders of the sun, that he did not notice a Golden Cloud come and settle down over the Garden, shedding a radiance a thousand times more brilliant than the sun itself, until, out of the cloud, a voice called,

"Adam! Adam!"

He turned towards the glowing Golden Cloud. The light dazzled him and he put up his hands to protect his eyes.

"Adam!" the voice called again.

Shielding his eyes from the glare, he looked again, and now he saw the two Archangels, one on either side of the cloud. It was Michael who had called his name.

"Adam, we are angels of the Creator. We have come to tell you that you will live on earth for one thousand years."

"Is that long or short?" Adam smiled timidly. "You must forgive my ignorance. I have been on earth only a few moments, as you know, and I cannot know whether one thousand years is long or short."

"For earth living," Gabriel said, "It is long, very long."

"Then I am satisfied," said Adam.

"You should be," said Michael. "But after you will come many who will not be as satisfied as you. They will not have your special blessing. They will not live as long as you. Most of your children's children will live on earth for only seventy or eighty years."

"Would you like to see the future generations?" asked Gabriel. "Would you like to see the people who will come after you?"

"Oh yes," Adam said. "Show me my children and my children's children."

"Come," said Gabriel. "Come to the Tree of Knowledge and thence to the Tree of Life. There you will see Noah and all the generations."

The two Angels led Adam towards the center of the Garden to the Tree of Knowledge. This tree was very tall and very wide, surrounded by hedges with heavy and thick foliage. As they came closer, Adam saw that within this hedge which surrounded the Tree of Knowledge was still another tree, the Tree of Life.

In order to get to the Tree of Life, a path had to be broken through the hedges surrounding the Tree of Knowledge. Adam, so newly born to life, could not have done this alone. But he had the Angels to help him.

They beat a way through the thorny thicknesses of ignorance. They threshed aside the heavy underbrush of stupidity. They scattered the rocky stones of laziness. And soon they began to show him the soft, easy path of intelligence. They began to trod the green grass of hard work. They walked down the pleasant paths of learning and then they came to the Tree of Knowledge. They stepped through the last hedge into a large, green clearing.

And there, before them, towered the Tree of Life.

The Tree of Life was rooted directly in the center of the clearing of the Tree of Knowledge. And beneath the Tree of Life flowed all the waters that irrigated the whole earth. These waters divided into four mighty streams, the Ganges, the Nile, the Tigris, and the Euphrates.

"Look now, Adam, upon the Tree of Life," Michael said.

As Adam looked, a white mist settled around the tree slowly blotting it out. Then the mist thickened and wove itself together to form a curtain. The misty whiteness began to change to gray, then green, then yellow and red. And from the colors a painted picture grew and in the picture figures began to form. And Adam gazed long at the moving pictures upon this Painted Curtain.

Then Adam saw David...

And he cried out, "No! No! Wait! Wait!"

"Do you see something on the Painted Curtain you do not like, Adam?" Michael asked.

Across it marched a pageant of people, led by Noah. Adam saw him stoop and rise and chop and hammer as he built the Ark. Then Adam watched the Flood waters sweep over the earth. He saw Abraham break the false idols of his father. He witnessed Esau sell his birthright for a mess of pottage, and old Isaac give the birthright blessing to Jacob. He studied the faces of Jacob's twelve sons and their tribes which were to become the twelve tribes of Israel. He watched how Joseph saved Egypt from starvation.

On the Painted Curtain marched the people of Israel on their long and difficult forty-year journey through the desert. Adam witnessed their disgrace as they fashioned the Golden Calf. He saw the manna which fell from heaven, and watched Moses receive the Torah on Mount Sinai. Then long wars paraded before his eyes, the wars with the Edomites and the Amalekites, of Og and Balak.

Then on the Painted Curtain he saw the people of Israel reach the Promised Land, and, passing in review were Joshua their leader, then Deborah, the Prophetess, Eli the Priest and Samuel the Prophet and Saul whom Samuel anointed as the first King of Israel.

"Look there, at David!" Adam exclaimed. "David is to have only three hours of life! That is not enough! He cannot achieve anything in three hours!"

"What do you think he should achieve?" Gabriel asked.

Adam spoke quickly. "David should be a great warrior, a mighty king, the sweet singer of Israel! There will be songs which he must compose, Psalms which he must sing to the glory of God. He cannot do all that in three short hours!"

"Ah yes." Michael nodded. "If David is to do all that you say, then surely three hours would not be sufficient. What then would you suggest?"

"Let me think," cried Adam. "Let me think." He covered his eyes with one hand and thought and thought. Finally he said,

"I know the answer, Michael. You say I shall have one thousand years of life. Let me give some of it to David."

"What will you give?"

"Seventy years," said Adam. "Nine hundred and thirty will be enough for me. Give the other seventy to David."

"That is a generous gift, Adam," Gabriel said. "To give years of your own life to another person is generous indeed."

"But I want to do it!" Adam exclaimed. "May I? May I give seventy years of my life to David?"

"It is a beautiful and an unselfish gift, Adam," said Michael. "You will be the only man in the whole world who will ever have the privilege of giving such a gift of life. There will be physicians on earth who will save people from dying too soon and thus add years to their life. But you are the only man whom the Lord will permit to give *away* any of his own years to another man. Are you sure you are willing?"

"Yes, I am willing!" Adam cried. "Give seventy years of my life to David!"

"Will you sign a contract to that effect?" Gabriel asked. "It is one thing to say you will do something nine hundred and thirty years in the future but another thing entirely to do it when the time comes. Will you sign a contract promising this gift?"

"Draw up the contract," Adam said impatiently. "Draw it up now. I will sign my name to it, and willingly."

"Very well," Michael said. "I shall call the heavenly Scribe." He called, "Metatron! Come, Metatron!"

The figures on the Painted Curtain began to merge and to fade. The colors began to dim, the bright reds cleared into pink and the brilliant greens faded to pale blues, and slowly all the colors were washed away until the Painted Curtain became gray, then white. The Curtain lost its thickness and its weave and its texture and wafted away into a mist which drifted off until the Tree of Life stood clearly revealed once more.

And now in front of the Tree of Life stood the angel Metatron by the side of Michael, holding a tablet made of gold and on it was writing in sapphire letters.

Metatron bowed his head slightly to Adam. "While you were thinking and talking, discussing and deciding, the Lord dictated this contract for me to write out, and here it is in the sapphire letters of heaven. The Lord of the world has already signed His Holy Name to it. I, as witness, have added mine. Now, Adam, before you sign your name, let me read it to you."

He held up the tablet and suddenly the Garden grew silent. In all of Eden not a bird chirped, not a leaf rustled, not a breeze stirred. No sound disturbed the hush. And the trees stood as silent, noble witnesses.

Metatron's clear, angel voice sounded out over the whole Garden as he read the Deed.

"I, Adam, hereby give and bequeath to David, son of Jesse, the Bethlehemite, seventy years of my life. Signed, this Sixth day of Creation, by the Most High; witnessed by the angel Metatron; and signed by myself, Adam, the first man on earth."

"Let me sign!" exclaimed Adam. "Let me sign at once!"

Metatron handed him a writing pen made of golden stone. It was long, and one end was pointed. As he wrote with it, out came sparkling sapphire dust to form the letters. Just as he began to write, he said,

"Thus to David do I give seventy years of my life. May he use those years well. May he be a wise king of Israel. May he always sing songs of praise to the Lord. Gladly do I give seventy years of my life to David, the Sweet Singer of Israel."

In sapphire dust, Adam signed his name to the golden tablet.

Thus was made the most precious gift that any man ever gave to another. Because of that gift, David lived to become a wise and noble king and wrote the Psalms, the most beautiful poetry the world has ever heard.

The Mystery of the Honey Jars

Long, long ago, in the town of Beth-lehem, lived Jesse and his eight sons. David was the youngest. His other brothers were so much older than he that they considered him a baby and paid very little attention to him. They went about their business and let him alone to amuse himself with his harp and his music.

One day as he was sitting in front of the open hearth in the big kitchen, David heard his father making plans for his brothers Eliab and Abinadab to go to Gilgal.

"King Saul," Jesse said, "is holding court at Gilgal. I want you to go there and present our case against neighbor Jethuel for stealing six of our sheep. Go and bring up the matter for King Saul's judgment."

"Very well, father," Eliab said. "This is a good time to go. It is the right season for a journey."

"Oh yes," agreed Abinadab. "In this dry season we can travel easily and quickly."

"Good," Jesse said. "Go now and prepare for your journey."

No one had paid any attention to young David as he sat on the hearth, plucking at his harp. When his father left the kitchen, and Eliab and Abinadab went outdoors,

David followed them to the stables. He sat down upon a rock and watched as they packed the donkeys with food for the journey and gifts for King Saul.

Abinadab, pausing for a moment in his work, saw David watching.

"Ho there, David," Abinadab said, then added teasingly, "I suppose you'd like to go with us, wouldn't you?"

"Oh yes!" David jumped to his feet. "May I?"

"Abinadab was only teasing," Eliab said roughly. "You would be in our way. No, you cannot go."

David's face fell.

"I *was* only teasing," Abinadab said. "But why not, Eliab? It would be a wonderful experience for David, and he won't be much trouble."

David's face brightened and he said quickly, "I won't be a nuisance. I promise."

"Very well, then," Eliab said gruffly, turning away. "You may come if our father gives his permission."

"Oh, thank you!"

He ran off to find his father.

"Oh father, father," he shouted. "May I? Please may I? They said I could if you say I may."

Jesse looked at him sternly. "You speak in riddles. Slow down. Stop stuttering. Who said what if I said which?"

David said more slowly, "Eliab and Abinadab said they will let me go to Gilgal with them if you will give me your permission."

Jesse looked thoughtfully at him.

"Would you promise to be of no trouble to Eliab and Abinadab?"

"Yes!"

"Would you obey your brothers?"

"Yes!"

"Would you behave in a way which befits a son of mine?"

"Yes!"

"Then you may go. I give you permission."

"Oh thank you, honored father. Thank you very much."

He ran to tell his brothers, then hurried to his mother to ask her to help him pack his clothes. And in a very short while, his harp slung across his back, he found himself astride his own small donkey, jogging down the dusty road alongside his two older brothers.

They had a long way to travel, starting from Beth-lehem, north to Jerusalem, then still farther north to Jericho and then on to Gilgal which was between Jericho and the Jordan River. Finally they arrived at King Saul's court.

The King knew their father and gave them a cordial reception. The royal court was in session and Eliab and Abinadab had to be present when their case was called. So David was sent to play with the King's children, Merab and Michal and Jonathan. Before very long all the children were good friends, and they played together for hours. But, while David romped with the boys and played music for the girls, he watched the excitement all around them. His eyes missed nothing.

This was the very day the law courts had opened and people streamed in from all over the kingdom, bringing their law suits before the King. Here was a man from Jerusalem whose neighbor had stolen two of his cows. There was a man from the farming country who had lost his entire wheat crop in a storm. All these people came, and many others, filling the courtyard with their donkeys and their mules and their wailing and their angry protests.

It was a colorful scene and exciting to David, a young shepherd lad whose life was spent with the quiet, slow moving sheep amongst the thorns and rocks of the pastures. This scene of bustling people in their many-colored garments, chattering in their many different accents, seemed at once strange and fascinating to him. And he watched them and listened to their complaints, wishing he could be inside at the court, never dreaming that serious-minded Jonathan was just as impatient as he.

Jonathan enjoyed listening to each case as it was presented, following both sides of an argument, trying to see if he would decide the case as his father would. It often happened that the King asked Jonathan's advice on a question in the law. But here he was outside the palace, and he really would much rather be inside.

The morning and early afternoon passed and now the crowd was beginning to thin. Finally Jonathan said to David,

"My father always lets me sit in the Court Room with him. Perhaps, if you promise to be quiet, he will let you sit with me."

"I'd like that!" David said.

"I'll ask him," Jonathan said, running off.

He returned in a few moments, told David to follow him quietly, and the two boys went into the Court Room. Doeg, King Saul's armor-bearer, met them at the door and told them to go quietly to their seats. Then he took up his usual position to the right of the King.

For the first few moments, David was so excited to find himself in King Saul's Court Room, he saw everything in a blur and heard the voices indistinctly. Then, when he became accustomed to the scene, he felt bold enough to look at King Saul who sat on his throne listening attentively to a case in which a man had been injured by his neighbor's ram. There were many people in the court, amongst them David's brothers, Eliab and Abinadab, whose case had already been heard.

The case about the man and the ram ended, and the Court Recorder called for the next case.

Up stepped a tall, handsome woman who was followed by two servants each carrying a large, heavy jar almost as big as the men themselves. The servants eased the two jars down on the floor, turned, bowed to the King, and backed away. Near the woman stood a small, thin man who smiled confidently. The woman came forward, bowed and said,

"Your Majesty, I have been robbed. And this man is the thief."

She turned and pointed her forefinger at the little thin man. He stepped forward and said loudly,

"O Your Majesty, she is mistaken. I am innocent."

"Proceed with your charge," King Saul said to the woman.

This was the story she told:

She was a rich woman, possessing many, many gold coins. A month ago it had been necessary for her to go on a long journey. It was impossible for her to take her money with her, and she was afraid to give it to anyone to keep for fear they would refuse to return it. Finally she decided on a good scheme. She divided the gold coins into two piles, and put each heap of gold at the bottom of a tall jar.

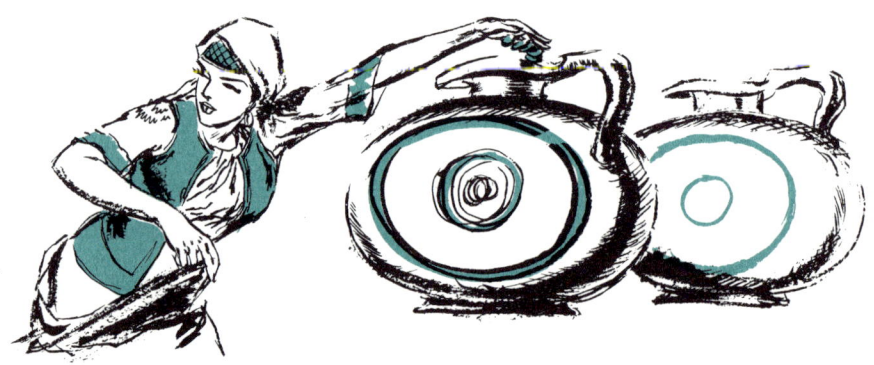

Then into these jars, covering the gold coins, she poured in thick, dark honey. And then no one could ever guess that there was anything in the jars but honey.

The woman pointed to the jars and said those were the jars into which she had put the gold and over which she had poured the honey. Then she had asked her neighbor, this thin man, to keep these jars of honey in his house while she was away from home. This he agreed to do.

She left on her journey, never thinking that her neighbor would guess that there was a fortune hidden in the honey. While she was gone, he must have discovered the money in the jars and had removed the gold. When she returned, he gave the jars back to her, filled with honey, but without the gold coins.

"Now," she said, concluding her complaint. "I want my money back."

King Saul turned to the thin man. "Did you take this woman's gold, as she says?"

"Oh no, Your Majesty," the thin man answered. "I never dreamed that there was anything in those jars but honey."

"What proof do you have that your neighbor took your money?" the King asked the woman.

"Who else could have taken it?" she said. "The money is gone. I put it in there, and he is the only one who could have taken it out."

"What proof have you that you put your money in the jars?" the King asked.

"Proof?" the woman asked, bewildered. "What proof can I offer? All I know is, I put the money there and now it is gone."

"Do not believe the woman, Your Majesty," the thin man said. "I returned the jars to her just as she gave them to me. I suggest, Your Majesty, that she has hidden her money somewhere else. And now she claims she put the gold in the honey-jars just to get *my* money away from me."

"That is not true," the woman cried. "You stole my money."

"Quiet, quiet," ordered the King. "I do not know whom to believe. Woman, the law is that he who makes a claim on his neighbor must bring the proof. You have no proof that you put the gold into the jars."

"No," she said sadly. "I have no proof. But I know I am telling the truth."

"But in law we need proof," the King said. "Have you any witnesses, then? Did any one *see* you put the money into the jars?"

"Oh no," she said tearfully. "I was careful that no one *should* see me."

"Did anyone see your neighbor *remove* the money from the jars?" the King asked.

"No," she admitted, shaking her head.

"Then, woman," King Saul said, "there are no witnesses and there is no proof. I cannot find this man guilty. We have no way of knowing that there ever was any money in these jars."

The woman started to cry and the little thin man smiled in triumph and began to turn away. Doeg leaned over and whispered to the King, and the King stopped the man.

"One moment. Before this case is dismissed, perhaps my son Jonathan has something to say."

Everyone turned to Jonathan who sat frowning at the little man. Then he said,

"This is a sad case, father. It seems to me the woman is telling the truth. It is too bad she hasn't any witnesses or any proof. I believe as you do, father, that although this man may well be guilty, we must do as you say, and let him go free."

Again the thin man smiled and turned away.

David leaned over to whisper to Jonathan. Doeg, noticing that, whispered into the King's ear.

"The young David seems to have an opinion."

The King smiled. "One moment," he said.

And the thin man came back to the throne.

Then the King, half teasingly, said to David,

"David, have you, perchance, an opinion on this case?"

David spoke up eagerly. "Yes, Your Majesty, if I may say just one thing."

King Saul and Doeg exchanged a smile, then the King said with mock seriousness,

"Most assuredly, David. You may speak."

"Your Majesty," David said. "I believe that there is proof that the woman put her money into the jars."

"Proof?" the King said. "What proof can there be, my boy?"

Doeg was no longer pleased with his little joke. He said sharply,

"Impudent boy. How can you find proof when King Saul himself and Jonathan cannot! They are both learned in the law, and you are a mere stripling. Do you think you are wiser than they?"

"Oh, no sir," David protested. "I am not wiser. But the woman has brought the proof with her. The jars of honey are her proof."

"Indeed," King Saul said. "In what way are these jars a proof?"

"May I whisper it to you?" David asked.

The King nodded and David stood up on the steps of the throne to reach the King's ear, and he whispered.

The King kept on nodding his head, then he said, "You may be right."

And he motioned to Doeg who bent his head, and the King whispered in his ear, and Doeg looked surprised.

"It may be. It may be," he said.

"So it may," said King Saul. Then he ordered, "Bring two hammers."

Doeg called for two servants. They came running forward with two hammers and, one, two, with two blows they cracked the jars. As the jars broke into pieces, there, sticking to a piece of the inside wall of the jars, were two gold coins!

"Proof!" the woman cried. "There is my proof!"

"Remarkable," Doeg murmured. "Truly remarkable. This David is a clever boy, a very clever boy."

David smiled, happy because now the woman would recover her money.

"Arrest that thief," King Saul ordered, pointing to the little, thin man.

Two guards sprang forward and grabbed the little man, who no longer smiled.

King Saul rose and said to the man, "Your carelessness has betrayed you. You are a fool and a thief. Take this thief to prison. Court is dismissed!"

The next day David left for home with his brothers. They were proud of their clever little brother. And he was proud of himself.

"I did obey you, didn't I?" he said to Eliab and Abinadab.

"Yes."

"And I did behave as befits a son of Jesse, didn't I?"

"Yes."

And all the way home to Beth-lehem he chattered about the wonderful things he had seen, and how he had decided a law case at the Court of King Saul.

The Stubborn Oil

David's boyhood was much like Joseph's, many centuries before. Like Joseph, David was a dreamer; and like Joseph, he was lonely.

Even his father Jesse was often puzzled at him because he was different from his brothers. They were practical men, living an every-day life, working and talking just like everyone else, while David was always writing poetry and singing songs. He even looked different from his brothers, with his fair skin and reddish hair. And so they felt that he was almost a stranger among them, and they often mocked him. But Jesse defended his youngest son. He would say to the older boys,

"Remember our ancestress, Miriam, the sister of Moses, and how she sang her songs at the Red Sea when our people fled from Egypt. Perhaps David has inherited Miriam's gift for music."

One day, David put aside his harp and and said to Jesse,

"Father, let me be a soldier like my brothers. Let me go to King Saul and become a warrior in his army."

"You?" Jesse laughed. "You a warrior? How would you hold a spear? As you hold your harp? No, keep to your songs, my son, and let your brothers sharpen their swords."

"No, I beg of you, father, listen to me," David said. "Some day I shall wage war against the Philistines. Some day I shall slay their giant, the mighty Goliath. Some day I shall build a Temple to God."

"A dreamer of dreams," Jesse said sadly, shaking his head, worried because such a person, a dreamer of dreams, surely could not protect himself in a world of wars and fierce fighting. He would have to guard David and keep him away from the world, close to home. And so Jesse said,

"No, my son, you will not join Saul's army. You will remain here in Bethlehem and tend the sheep."

David pretended to be content with this arrangement, and he became the shepherd of Jesse's flocks. It was an easy task except of course when wild animals attacked the sheep. Then David beat them off, glad of the chance to prove at least to himself how brave he really was. Otherwise, it was true, he could play his harp and sing his songs, and he had many songs to sing and new ones to compose. So he protected his flocks and created his music. He seemed satisfied and life moved smoothly along.

Then, one day, the old Prophet Samuel came to Beth-lehem.

Eliab, Jesse's eldest son, who was at the market-place, saw him first. Forgetting his business at the market, he rushed home to bring the news to his father.

"Father, I have just come from the market-place. Samuel is here in Beth-lehem."

"Samuel, the Prophet of Israel?" Jesse asked. "Call my sons together. This visit may concern our household."

Eliab rushed away to summon his brothers, and in a few moments seven of them gathered around their father in the hall of cedarwood.

"I do not see David," Jesse said.

"Oh, I didn't bother to call him away from the sheep," Eliab said carelessly.

Jesse nodded. "If we should need him, he isn't far away." Then he motioned for quiet.

"Listen, my sons. Samuel, the Prophet of Israel, once did great honor to the House of Kish of the tribe of Benjamin. He anointed Saul, the son of Kish, as the first King of Israel. Perhaps Samuel comes now to confer some honor on the House of Jesse. Conduct yourselves nobly, my sons. Conduct yourselves as true descendants of Miriam."

When Jesse stopped speaking, all the brothers began talking at once. But Shammah's voice rose above the rest.

"Father, I think we should send for David."

"Oh, David," Abinadab said. "Leave him alone with his songs and his dreams."

Then Eliab posted himself at the door to watch for Samuel. After a few moments, he whispered,

"He is here! Samuel is here!"

Jesse, followed by his seven sons, stepped through the door and walked a few paces toward Samuel, and they all bowed low. Jesse said,

"Welcome, Samuel. Welcome, Prophet of Israel. You honor the House of Jesse as you come under the shadow of his roof."

"May peace abide in the House of Jesse," Samuel said. "You rejoice my heart with your welcome."

He greeted each son, Eliab, Abinadab, Shammah and the others.

Samuel and Jesse entered the house, the brothers following. Jesse led the way into the hall of cedarwood and up to a couch and invited Samuel to be seated. Samuel turned and looked again at each son as if counting them, and shook his head.

"I see only seven sons, Jesse," he said. "Have you not eight sons?"

"Oh yes," Jesse said quickly. "David is the eighth. He is in the pasture with the sheep. But come, Samuel, sit down and rest. You must be weary from your travels."

"I have no time to rest, Jesse," Samuel answered. "I have come to Bethlehem on a secret journey, with a secret mission. Until that mission is accomplished, I may not rest. So send for your son David, Jesse, that I may complete my task.

Jesse smiled. "You will find no need for my son David. He is a light-minded lad who sings songs and dreams of the grand things that will happen to him in the future."

"Oh leave David alone with his harp," Eliab said. "His music and the sheep are all that he cares about."

"Very well," Samuel said.

He was satisfied. He was attracted to Eliab and believed that his mission to

Jesse's house might well concern this tall, strong eldest son. He turned to Jesse and began to speak.

"Jesse, I come on a matter of greatest importance. So listen carefully."

He looked from Jesse to Eliab, and continued,

"Saul is King of Israel. When he dies, the House of Saul will be finished. His crown will not go to one of his sons. When Saul dies, the next King of Israel will come——" he paused and said slowly, "from the House of Jesse."

"From my House!" Jesse exclaimed. "O Samuel, oh, this is a great honor. Which of my sons will you choose to be King after Saul?"

"That we shall soon see," Samuel said. "The future King will be anointed with oil."

He put his hand into his pouch and drew out a horn made from an elephant's tusk, and then he pulled out small bundles of herbs wrapped in linen and a mortar and pestle. He put all the herbs into the bowl and pounded and rubbed and mixed them all together into one heap of fine powder and on that he poured some sweet-smelling oil.

Then he turned his back on everyone and secretively took one last thing out of the pouch and dropped it into the bowl.

He turned back to Jesse and said,

"Now I have prepared the holy oil with which I shall anoint him who shall some day be King of Israel."

He held the horn of ivory in one hand and with the other he lifted the mortar and poured the oil from it into the tusk. As it flowed in, a thin veil of smoke rose from the horn towards heaven.

"This rising smoke," he said, "is caused by a special secret herb."

He held the horn of oil in his right hand, and said,

"Eliab, come thou forward."

Eliab took two steps forward and stood in front of Samuel.

Samuel lifted the horn of ivory containing the holy oil, and said,

"I, Samuel, Prophet of Israel, anoint thee, Eliab, King of Israel."

He tried to pour oil from the horn onto Eliab's head. But nothing happened! Not a drop of oil squeezed out. Samuel shook the horn, and shook it, but still no oil flowed, and the smile on Eliab's face gave way to a frown. Everyone looked dismayed except Abinadab who was the next eldest son. He began to smile.

Samuel said, "Abinadab, come thou forward."

Eliab stepped back. Abinadab stepped forward. Samuel held the horn of oil over the head of Abinadab.

"I, Samuel, Prophet of Israel, anoint thee, Abinadab, King of Israel."

Abinadab smiled. Samuel shook the horn. Again nothing happened. The oil did not flow. Samuel shook it again. Not a droplet of oil came out. Abinadab's smile turned to a frown.

And now the third son, Shammah, began to smile. He raised his head high and waited impatiently for Samuel to anoint him with oil.

Jesse and the other brothers watched anxiously as Samuel turned away from Abinadab to Shammah, then from Shammah to the fourth brother, to the fifth, the sixth and finally to the seventh brother. But when the oil still did not run from the horn over the seventh brother, everyone was filled with gloom.

Surely there must be something wrong with the oil. Surely there must be something wrong with the way Samuel tilted the horn.

"Samuel," Jesse said sharply. "You must have forgotten to add the secret ingredient to make the oil holy."

"I did not forget," Samuel answered sternly.

All the men were frowning but none as fiercely as Samuel. Now he spoke again to Jesse and his voice was harsh and stern.

"God has sent me to anoint a son of Jesse. You have yet one more son. Send for him. Send for David!"

"David!" Eliab said scornfully. "David indeed! Do you think the oil will pour for David if it did not pour for us? For David, the music maker?"

"For David?" scoffed Shammah. "For David, the plucker of the harp?"

"He is the least of us," the other brothers said.

Samuel silenced them all with one stern look. "I have been sent to anoint a son of the House of Jesse. Send for the boy David."

Jesse did not argue. He sent Shammah to call his younger brother in from the fields.

As Shammah reached the pasture, he heard David singing, and a moment later, his harp slung across his back, his shepherd's scrip hanging from his belt, David came in sight. His head was thrown back, his mouth open as he flung his song to the skies so happily, so merry-hearted that for a moment Shammah envied him. Then he remembered he was only a shepherd, and he called out roughly,

"Hurry there, David. Our father wants you."

David saw his brother and began to run towards him. "Shammah! What an adventure I have had! A most exciting adventure! Today while I was watching the sheep I climbed what I thought was a little hill. But it wasn't a hill! It was a huge animal, a Re'em, a great, enormous Re'em, asleep, sound asleep. But as soon as he felt me on his back, he awoke and began to rear up, ready to dash me to pieces! There I was on the back of the Re'em . . . when suddenly from out of the forest came a lion, and when the Re'em saw the king of beasts it prostrated itself. It bowed down, and you can imagine that I speeded, quick as the wind, off its back. And then! — and then the lion turned to attack me and to devour me."

"What did you do?" shouted Shammah, excited in spite of himself.

"I just held my breath and prayed to God," David said. "And God sent a deer bounding out of the forest. When the lion saw the deer, away he went in pursuit of the poor deer. And I was safe!"

"Oh, you made up the whole story," Shammah said grumpily. "Enough of your foolishness. Hurry along now. We have no time for these idle dreams of yours. We have a noble visitor."

But David did not listen. "And then I had another adventure, Shammah."

Now they reached the house and as they entered, David was still talking.

"A band of wild beasts attacked my sheep. I had no weapons at all. You know I never carry weapons, just my bare hands, and with my bare hands I killed those beasts, Shammah, four lions and three bears, and I saved all my sheep. Not one ewe lamb was harmed."

"Cease your idle chatter, David," Jesse commanded. "Do you not see we have an honored guest?"

David spun around and recognized the guest. "The Prophet Samuel! O forgive me. I did not see you. I was so busy telling my brothers of my adventures. Welcome to my father's house."

"Indeed, is this David?" Samuel looked the boy over.

And, of course, David did not look too attractive just then, coming in from the warm fields, his shepherd's robes wrinkled and grass-stained. But his face was smiling and his eyes were happy. Samuel did not look at his face, only at his wrinkled garments, and he said, gloomily,

"I have come to anoint the future King of Israel from the House of Jesse."

"A King!" David exclaimed. "One of my brothers is to be King! How wonderful. Which one?"

"Hush lad," Abinadab said crossly. "We do not know yet."

"Quiet now, all of you," Jesse said.

Only David had trouble controlling his excitement. The other brothers stood about glumly, frowning, staring at the floor. David was smiling, looking with lively interest from Samuel, to the horn in his hand, to Jesse, to each of the brothers. He shifted from foot to foot, eager and impatient to see which brother Samuel would choose.

"Now that all my sons are here," Jesse said, "begin again, O Prophet. Begin with the eldest."

Samuel said, "Eliab, come thou forward."

Eliab obeyed.

"I, Samuel, Prophet of Israel, anoint thee, Eliab, King of Israel."

Once more Samuel tried to pour oil on Eliab, but no oil flowed. Then he tried to anoint Abinadab and Shammah and all the other brothers. And again the stubborn oil stayed fast in the horn. And on each brother's face the scowls deepened as their disappointment mounted, and Jesse sighed more and more unhappily.

Then Samuel turned to David, but Jesse said,

"What is the use of trying David? Would God reject these fine, soldierly sons for this shepherd?"

"Who knows God's purpose?" Samuel answered. "His thoughts are not our thoughts. Man looketh at the outer form but God looketh at the heart. We shall see if perhaps David is the one."

"I?" David's face beamed, then grew quickly serious. He stood motionless as if holding his breath, his eyes wide in astonishment, his hands stiff at his side.

"I, Samuel, Prophet of Israel, anoint thee, David, King of Israel."

Before Samuel finished these words, the oil began to run smoothly, slowly from the horn, over David's head, onto his shoulders, and over his garments. And as each drop clung to his robe, it glistened like diamonds and pearls, and still the horn was full of oil.

"It is David," Samuel's voice boomed out. "It is David who is God's chosen one, God's anointed. He will be King in Israel after Saul!"

"I will sing a song unto the Lord!" David cried. And he sang:—
> *"This is the day which the Lord hath made,*
> *We will rejoice and be glad in it."*

Thus David, the despised youngest brother, the singer of songs, the keeper of the flocks, was anointed by Samuel to be the future King of Israel.

The King's Armor

King Saul was at war with the Philistines. The enemy was encamped in Ephes-dammim, and Saul's camp was in the Vale of Elah. There the thousands of warriors of the tribes of Benjamin and Judah and other tribes were encamped. And amongst them, from Beth-lehem in Judah, were David's three brothers, Eliab and Abinadab and Shammah.

One day, David's father said to him,

"Your brothers are in need of provisions. Go thou, and take them corn and bread and cheeses. Prepare to leave immediately."

David went quickly about his preparations, changing into clean clothes, loading the donkey with the provisions. He slung his harp across his back, secured his scrip-pouch to his belt, and off he rode to the wars.

He travelled hard and fast, impatient to get to Saul's army, sure the war would be over before his balky donkey could reach Elah. Over hill, down dale he went, across mountains, wading into streams with rocky bottoms, onto green grass again, until finally he reached the Valley of Elah.

His brothers greeted him happily. Their provisions were getting low and they needed the corn and bread and cheeses he brought from Beth-lehem. And he brought news from home and they were glad to see him.

While they were unpacking the donkey, David kept looking around at the army camp. What he saw in the camp surprised him.

He pulled at his brother's sleeve. "Eliab, what is wrong with the men? They look frightened and angry, not like brave soldiers. Their clothes are unwashed and their swords unpolished. What kind of an army is this?"

"Oh, it's a good enough army." Eliab fingered his own uncombed hair. "But we're in trouble."

"Well, of course," David said impatiently. "Every army is always in trouble. You have an enemy to fight. If you're a soldier you're always in danger . . ."

"No, no," Shammah interrupted. "We are in special trouble. The soldiers are down-hearted because we are faced with sure defeat. We have no chance to win. We are going to be defeated without flinging a single javelin, without thrusting a single sword."

"What do you mean?" David said irritably. "Why do you speak of defeat? Why will you not fight? Where are your generals? Where is King Saul?"

"Oh, we have generals enough," Abinadab said, and sighed. "We have Abner and Jonathan and Doeg, brave and courageous warriors. But in this trouble, no, there is nothing they can do. They are powerless."

Drawn by the sound of voices, other soldiers began to edge close to the group. More and more men came to sit on the ground, listening gloomily. Shammah said,

"Listen, David. In the Philistine army there is a famous soldier, nay, a giant of a soldier whose name is Goliath. This one soldier, this giant Goliath, threatens to destroy the whole of King Saul's army."

"One soldier?" David asked, astonished. "One soldier will destroy you, all of you? And you won't even fight back?"

"Listen, brother," Eliab said. "It has been decided in the council of generals that there is only one man who can fight this giant, this Goliath. And that one man is the man who can wear the armor of the King."

"That means King Saul himself," David said quickly. "Very well, then, why doesn't King Saul go and do battle with Goliath?"

"Alas, the King is sick."

Every man hung his head, and sighed.

"The King is sick. King Saul is very sick. Too sick to fight. Too sick to wear his armor."

"Then his generals . . ." David stammered eagerly. "I have heard how strong Abner is. Surely the mighty Abner could put on the King's armor and destroy this giant Philistine."

"No." Abinadab shook his head. "No, not even Abner. Nor Jonathan, nor Doeg. They have all tried to put on King Saul's armor. It will not fit any one of them. It will fit no man in the army."

"Surely, oh surely there must be one man in the army," David insisted. "There must be one man who would fit into the King's armor."

All the men looked at each other uneasily, then away, murmuring a little, drawing slightly back from David.

One man muttered, "Who would dare try? Who wants to fight the giant? It would mean death. No one in the army dares try it."

"But," David said, "perhaps there is a man not yet in the army . . ."

"Even so," muttered Eliab. "It would be dangerous, too dangerous. Only a miracle can save us now."

David nodded. "Yes, a miracle. The Lord has performed miracles for His people many times. Maybe now He will send another miracle. And if He did, and if one man engages in battle with this giant and defeats this Goliath, tell me, what would be his reward from the King?"

Some one laughed, sharply, quickly. One man said,

"That would be a lucky man indeed. Saul would give him great wealth, and the princess, his daughter, for a wife, and secure the protection of his father's house."

Everyone fell silent, but David unslung his harp from his back, began to pluck the strings. Then softly he began to sing, his clear voice sounding out like a bell in the deep silence of the army camp. No one stirred. The breeze ruffled the leaves on the trees. Otherwise there was silence broken only by the sound of David's beautiful voice singing song after song.

The men began to relax, leaning on their elbows, listening to the music, dreaming of home. An air of peace fell over them.

Suddenly into the group strode Abner, the General. The men jumped to their feet and saluted. David let a single clear note fade off.

"I heard the music," Abner said. He looked keenly at David. "And I see how these troubled men were soothed by it. Perhaps," he said thoughtfully, "perhaps with your music you can also ease the troubled spirit of the King."

"If I can," David said quietly, "I would be glad to. Music does ease a man's sickness, I know."

"Then, young man, come with me." said Abner.

David rose and walked with Abner, who said, "The King is ill, but not with an

illness of the body. It is a sickness of the mind which torments him. Would you be fearful of his outcries and perhaps of his violence?"

"No," David said. "I would feel pity but no fear."

The two men walked through the camp until they reached the clearing in front of the King's tent. Six soldiers stood guard. The head guard, seeing Abner, stepped aside, and Abner and David walked into the gloom of the King's tent.

Prince Jonathan stood to one side, his head bowed. Doeg stood on the other side, his piercing eyes observing David's entrance into the tent. The King's servants were hurrying noiselessly to and fro, bringing wine for his parched lips, soft cloths for his fevered brow, fans to move the heavy air away from his head.

The King himself half sat, half lay across his throne. He moaned, moving his head restlessly from side to side. Then suddenly he cried out, and opened his eyes, then shut them quickly as if even the faint light of the tent sent quivers of pain along his temples. He groaned, and twisted his hands, murmuring foolish words, then shouting battle commands.

Abner motioned to David to sit over in the corner out of sight. David crept to the far end of the tent next to a carved chest, seated himself cross-legged on the thick carpet, and unslung his harp.

A servant approached the King and offered him wine. Saul groaned and dashed the winecup to the ground. The servant backed away.

David plucked one string of his harp, and then another, and soon a ripple of melody stirred the air.

The tent grew still. All noise stopped except for the moaning of the King and the plucking of David's harp. Then, taking courage, David began to sing, very softly at first, then louder, then still louder until soon the sweet music filled the tent. It reached the King's ears. He dug his head deep into a pillow as if to escape the song.

David kept on singing. It was a quiet song, a sweet one, with the pleasant background harmony of the strumming of the harp. The King's breathing began to be easier, less labored. An attendant wiped his forehead with a soft wet cloth. Another stroked his wrists and one servant held a cup of wine to his lips. The King sipped the wine, leaned his head back, closed his eyes. And all the while David's sweet music filled the air.

Then, with a long, shuddering breath and a deep sigh, the King fell asleep!

Jonathan and Doeg and Abner looked at each other in surprise. But no one uttered a word. David's harp gave forth one last tender note and then his fingers flattened against the strings, stilling the hum.

"The King sleeps! The King sleeps!"

Throughout the tent one person whispered to another. Jonathan turned to David with a look of surprised thanks in his eyes.

The King's sleep did not last long, perhaps not more than a half hour. When he awoke, he awoke refreshed. His eyes were clear and his voice was firm.

He lifted his head slowly from the pillow, looked at his son Jonathan, then at his generals, Abner and Doeg, and then his sharp eyes pierced through the gloom to the corner where David sat cross-legged, his harp resting on his knees. The King raised his hand slowly, crooked his forefinger and beckoned to David to come forward.

David sprang to his feet, slinging his harp across his back, and walked to the King. Reaching the throne, he kneeled. Saul touched his head lightly with two fingers.

"Rise and receive my thanks for your healing music."

"May God grant health to you, O King," David said quietly, rising.

"What is your name? And who is your father?"

"My father is Jesse of Beth-lehem. And I am David, his youngest son."

Jonathan broke in. "Surely, O Father, you remember David? When he was but a boy, he sat in your court and helped you decide the case of the gold in the honey jars."

David smiled.

"Ah, indeed, I remember," King Saul said. "And now today you help me again. Your service to me shall not go unrewarded. You shall become my armor-bearer."

Before David could voice his thanks, the King had turned to his son Jonathan. He said,

"Jonathan, O my son. This lad with his music has relieved my sickness. But still my body has not enough strength for battle. And Goliath waits to destroy us. Is there no one to help us?"

Then Jonathan said, "Let us try again. Surely your suit of armor will fit one of us. Doeg, Abner." He turned to the two generals. "Come, let us try once more to wear my father's armor."

Neither Abner nor Doeg protested, though they knew it was useless. They waited while the King's former armor-bearer brought the helmet of brass, the coat of mail and the sword. He handed them first to Jonathan.

Now Jonathan was as tall as his father, but not as broad of shoulder. The helmet of brass slipped down over his head and the coat of mail hung loosely upon him. With a regretful sigh, he lifted off the helmet, then the coat of mail and handed it to Doeg.

Doeg was broad enough but much too short. It took only one glance to see that he could never wear the coat of mail. Silently he handed the brass helmet to Abner who took it and held it in his hand, a look of helplessness on his face.

Abner was in all truth a giant. He was very tall and very broad and very wide. And indeed he was much too large for the armor. The brass helmet sat on the top of his head like a little cap. And he didn't even try to put on the coat of mail. He couldn't even get it over his shoulders.

The King shook his head. "No one," he murmured. "It fits no one."

Then, to everyone's astonishment, young David spoke up.

"Please, O King," he said. "Forgive my boldness. But would Your Majesty permit me to try on the King's armor?"

"You?" the King asked and smiled.

Abner almost laughed out loud. But David said seriously,

"Yes, Your Majesty. Let me try. There can be no harm in trying."

"That's true," Jonathan spoke up quickly. "He can at least try."

"Look how slender he is," Abner said, controlling his laughter. "It would never fit him, never. It would be a miracle if it did."

"Such impudence," Doeg grumbled. "This unknown shepherd lad presuming to wear the King's armor! Impudence."

"No, no," King Saul said impatiently, moving his head from side to side. "He means no impudence. Indeed, Jonathan is right. What harm can there be? Yes, David, my lad, you may try on the King's armor and perhaps by some chance it will fit you."

David unslung his harp and handed it to Jonathan. Then, as he began to put on the coat of mail, Doeg and Abner began to laugh, and even the King smiled, though kindly.

The coat of mail hung on David's shoulders like a loose sack of metal.

But suddenly everyone straightened up, hardly believing what they were seeing!

The mail coat had begun to shrink! It shrank down and shrank up and it shrank in. There was a soft grinding sound and a gentle clashing of chain as the pieces slid over each other. And, as they watched, the metal eased itself onto David's shoulders and levelled off to his arms. It drew in towards his body and clung to his chest and fitted in to his waist. Within just a few moments, it fit David as perfectly as if it had been made for him.

The King's smile faded. Doeg and Abner stopped laughing. Jonathan, a puzzled frown on his forehead, handed David the helmet of brass.

David raised his arms slowly because of the weight of the mail coat, put the helmet on his head. And once again the King smiled and Doeg and Abner laughed when the helmet fell over David's head like a sack. But once again their amusement vanished when miraculously, like the coat, the helmet shrank until soon it fit David's head as perfectly as ever it had fit Saul's.

"It is a miracle, O King," said Abner. "A miracle, indeed."

"Indeed," Jonathan said quietly. "Now wondrously the armor fits young David, my father."

"Yes, it fits me, Your Highness," David said eagerly. "Now I ask only your permission. Let me go. Let me battle the giant Goliath."

The King protested. "But, David, you are only a lad."

"But we know that the Lord is with him," Jonathan said.

"Yes, the Lord is with me," David said. "He has always been with me and helped me to protect my flocks. I have slain many a wild beast while guarding my sheep. And with God's help I can slay Goliath too. I seek only your permission to go."

Saul looked at him long and earnestly. Then he said,

"The armor fits you well. Therefore, I, Saul, the King, grant you permission. Go thou, David, in the armor of the King of Israel. Go forth! Battle the giant Goliath!"

The Five Pebbles

For three days the giant Goliath had been mocking the armies of Israel. Each day he walked out of the camp of the Philistines and stood between the two armies, shouting his insults. In his impudence, he even challenged the God of Israel to do battle with him. Now that was great impudence indeed.

Goliath *must* be slain. But, only one man could fight the giant, and that was King Saul himself. But King Saul was ill. His soldiers knew that if a man could be found who was big enough and strong enough to wear the King's armor, that man too could fight Goliath. But none of Saul's generals could wear his armor, not his son Jonathan, nor Abner, nor Doeg.

Then along had come the shepherd lad, David. He tried on the clanking suit of mail and, as all the army knew by now, miraculously, the armor shrank until, lo! — it fitted him!

Now, wearing the King's armor which had so wondrously shrunk, David stood confidently in front of King Saul. Everyone in the royal tent knew that now he could go out to battle with the giant Goliath. And everyone was relieved, except Doeg.

He had discovered somehow that the Prophet Samuel had secretly anointed David as King to rule after Saul. And this did not suit Doeg at all. Ever since the King fell sick, more and more power had been given over to Doeg. If Jonathan were to rule after Saul, Doeg would continue to hold his favored position in

37

the King's court. But now, since David had been selected to be Saul's successor, it would ruin Doeg's chances for gaining more and more power. So Doeg determined to put this young man out of the way as quickly as possible.

He did not join those who crowded around David, congratulating him for being able to wear the King's armor, advising him how to battle Goliath. Instead, Doeg leaned over the throne, whispering to King Saul.

"Hear me, my Master. This young David is a dangerous man. Some day he will plot against you. He will hunt for your very life. He will lay traps and kill you. And he will slay your son Jonathan, and then this David will rule as King over Israel."

Having planted this seed of suspicion in the King's sick mind to arouse his fears, Doeg now began to awaken the King's jealousy. He pretended to praise David.

"But perhaps, after all, he *is* fit to be King, O Saul. Look at his handsome face. See his strong, healthy body."

King Saul turned his sick and tired eyes on David and studied him. And Doeg whispered into the King's ear,

"He sings so beautifully, O King. His voice is tender and his hand upon the harp strings is sure. David is a man of poetry and music. Ah yes, perhaps young David is indeed a man suited to be King."

Then Doeg delivered the climax of his praise.

"His mind, too, O King, is well trained. It is sharp and keen and well versed in the law. Indeed I have heard high praise of his knowledge. He will make a wise King, a very wise King indeed."

Saul was glaring in rage at David. Doeg stepped back from the throne, satisfied that his poisonous words were taking effect.

A short while ago Saul had been thanking David for his healing music, admiring him for fitting into the armor. And now he looked at him as if he were his greatest enemy. He frowned, and his eyes flashed with suspicion.

Now David was not so busy being fawned on and congratulated that he did not see all these things. He observed how Doeg whispered to the King. He saw the smile leave the King's face and the frown replace it. He saw the flashing looks of suspicion and the glares of rage. And David realized that King Saul was suddenly jealous of him because he could wear the King's armor and go fight the enemy whom the King himself was too ill to fight.

Quickly, but politely, without being rude to the people exclaiming over him, David turned to the King and made a stiff bow. Then quietly he said,

"Your Majesty, if I may be permitted to speak."

The King gave a sign.

David continued. "I am ready now, O King, to go and do battle with Goliath. But, with Your Majesty's permission, I would like to take off this royal suit of armor."

A murmur spread through the tent. King Saul, the scowl on his face fading slowly, said,

"Why does the King's own armor not suit young David?"

And David answered, "Your Majesty, the King's armor honors me but it is too grand for me. It is foolish for me to imagine that I can take the place of the great King Saul just by wearing his armor. No, Your Majesty. I am a shepherd, and, as a shepherd, in shepherd's garb, I shall fight Goliath."

The King's face brightened up and, as he smiled, Doeg frowned, furious that the King had been won over by David's soft and simple words.

David tried to step forward, but he stumbled. He turned to the King.

"You see, Your Majesty. I can scarcely move in this armor. It is splendid, but heavy. I have not been trained to wear garments worthy of a King. Let me fight Goliath in my own shepherd's clothing."

He began to lift off the brass helmet, and the King said approvingly,

"The young man speaks modestly and wisely. Help him remove the armor."

"But Your Majesty," blurted Doeg. "He cannot fight Goliath without your armor. If he fights without a mail coat, Goliath will indeed be scornful of King Saul who sends a mere lad to fight a giant. But if he wears the King's armor, perhaps Goliath will be fooled into thinking he is fighting King Saul."

David smiled. "No one can pretend to be King Saul. Wearing a King's armor does not make a man a King. I shall fight as well as I can without armor."

"No, my father," Jonathan broke in, protesting. "Do not permit it. It is too dangerous. David must have the protection of armor, or Goliath will kill him before he can defend himself."

"I can defend myself." David said, removing the coat of mail.

"Yes, yes," the King said irritably. "He can defend himself."

"Of course," Doeg said smoothly. "David can still refuse to fight Goliath."

"No," David answered quickly. "Goliath has insulted the armies of Israel and mocked God himself. We *must* fight Goliath and destroy him."

Doeg said nothing more. He was satisfied, confident that David, unprotected by armor, would be slain by the giant with one thrust of his sword.

David hung his slingshot from his wrist, slung his harp across his shoulders, took his staff in hand. He bowed to the King.

"O King, with your permission, I leave. Give me your blessing, O King of Israel."

"Go, David," the King said restlessly. "Go, with my blessing. Go, and return victorious."

David bowed again, turned and left the royal tent. Behind him came Jonathan and Abner and Doeg, with their armor-bearers. As these men followed David through the camp, some soldiers joined the procession. David marched through the forest to the foot of the hills, and more and more soldiers fell into step behind him.

He stopped only once, at the foot of a hill at a small brook running lazily over smooth stones. He stooped and gathered five pebbles into his hand. From his belt he took a knife and on each of the five stones he scratched the names of Abraham and Isaac, Jacob and Moses and Aaron. And then, in addition, he scratched on each stone the Name of the Almighty. He returned the knife to his belt and then put the stones carefully into his pouch. He stood up and continued onward and upward to the top of the hill overlooking the Vale of Elah.

There on the summit he stopped and looked across to the next hill. Goliath stood there, dangerously close.

He was truly a giant, and a very fearful-looking giant was he. In his hand he carried a tremendous spear, the spearhead made of heavy iron. On his head he wore a helmet of brass, on his legs greaves of brass, and a javelin of brass was fastened between his shoulders. He was a giant in shining brass, and the sight of him struck terror into every man who had climbed up behind David.

"David, turn back!" Abner exclaimed. "You cannot battle this giant. Goliath wears more than one suit of armor. It would be impossible to pierce him even with the heaviest spear! Turn back, David, turn back."

"True," Doeg murmured insincerely, secretly pleased. "And David is completely unprotected. Of course, only a coward would turn back now. Still, David, perhaps you'd better not try. You'll most certainly be killed."

"Turn back, David," Jonathan pleaded. "Turn back."

But David answered no one. He stood with his legs spread apart, his hands on his hips, calmly looking at the giant. Goliath did not look calmly at David, but with contempt. And then he laughed. He laughed again, then looked scornfully at the staff David held in his right hand. But suddenly Goliath stopped laughing. Becoming angry, he shouted,

"Am I a dog, that you come to fight me with a staff?"

David shouted back, "You come well armed, Goliath, with a sword and a javelin and a spear. But I come better armed. I come in the Name of the Lord of Hosts."

"The Lord of Hosts," sneered Goliath, and began to move forward, raising his arm to throw his javelin. "You're nothing but a weakling."

At that moment, the Angel Zeruel appeared at David's side.

"I am Zeruel, the Angel of Strength, O David. I have come to give you strength."

Goliath moved forward another step, the javelin poised for the throw.

But suddenly—suddenly David threw one look at him—and that look rooted Goliath to the ground!

"Now your strength is complete," the Angel Zeruel said. "Fight well, O David. The Lord is with you."

And the Angel Zeruel vanished.

Goliath was rooted in helplessness. He strained and strained and could not budge an inch. He could not move. Angered at his sudden weakness, he began shouting taunts at David.

"Is King Saul so poor he had no one to send but a stripling like you?"

David didn't answer and Goliath raged, struggling to get free. David put his hand into the pouch and took out the five pebbles. Goliath, enraged though he was, began to laugh.

"Ho!" he shouted. "Do you think to vanquish me with those pebbles? Am I a sparrow? Ho, ho!"

David rolled the five pebbles in his fingers. His hands moved slowly, turning and twisting, rubbing the five stones against each other. And then the pebbles began to join together, to melt into each other, to become bigger and bigger and suddenly they merged together to form one large stone! He removed the slingshot from his wrist, fitted the stone in it, and looked across at Goliath.

Goliath strained to get free, and raged at David.

"Come thou but nearer and I will strike you with one blow," he shouted. "I will tear your body and feed it to the beasts of the field."

"I will feed your body to the fowl of the air," David shouted back.

And he looked up into the sky.

Goliath, thinking there were buzzards flying above him, looked overhead, and, as he did, the vizor of his helmet sprang open.

David took aim, and his slingshot released the huge stone and zinggggg... it whizzed across the distance, flying with sure aim. And it struck Goliath right between the eyes, killing him instantly.

Slowly he collapsed to the ground. The weight of his armor dragged him down and clanked noisily around the body of the dead giant. Thus he lay, forever silent, slain by the young shepherd lad, David, who slew him with a stone.

"Goliath is dead!" Jonathan yelled.

"Our enemy is beaten!" Abner shouted.

"Hurrah! Victory!"

The voices of the men rang across the hills, into the valley, the echoes reaching into the camp of Israel.

Only Doeg was silent.

After a while David turned his back on the dead Goliath and marched back down the hill to King Saul's tent. Jonathan marched with him, escorting him right to his father's throne.

"David returns victor," cried Jonathan. "O my father, the wicked Goliath is slain."

Doeg was right behind him, looking blackly angry. But King Saul paid no attention to Doeg's jealous murmurings.

"Welcome, our brave warrior!" the King exclaimed as David bowed before him. "Welcome to my court. Welcome to the family of Saul. To you shall I give my daughter Michal in marriage. Welcome, David. Welcome, my son."

Thus did the shepherd lad, David, move up from the pastures to the royal court, from his father's house to King Saul's palace. He and Michal were joined in marriage. And he became like a son to King Saul and like a brother to Jonathan.

David and the Spider

For many years David protected his flocks against wild beasts. Then he pursued the Philistines, enemies of Israel. But the day came when David learned how it felt to be not the hunter but the hunted; not the pursuer but the pursued.

After joining Saul's army, his life was successful and happy. He rose quickly from being the King's armor-bearer to the position of an honored general, for David soon showed himself trustworthy in battle, brave, fearless and completely loyal to the King. Saul grew to love him almost as much as his own son Jonathan and he invited David to join his household. After living at the King's court a short time, David married the King's daughter, Michal.

Having risen so steadily in the King's favor, David thought that his position was secure. But he reckoned without the King's sick mind which could easily be swayed by jealousy.

Now King Saul had always taken it for granted that his son Jonathan would rule as King after him. But, shortly after David married Michal, the Prophet Samuel informed Saul that his son Jonathan would never rule as King of Israel. Samuel said that the Lord had decided that the King after Saul would be David, the son of Jesse, the Beth-lehemite.

That was the beginning of Saul's hatred of David.

Doeg, one of the King's counsellors, was the first to guess that the King's affections for David had turned to mistrust. Doeg had long been jealous of David and was quick to use the turn of affairs to suit himself. His plan was to destroy completely the King's faith in David by increasing the King's anger day by day.

This he did cunningly. Instead of finding fault or trying to belittle David in the King's eyes, Doeg did the opposite. He praised David. He praised him constantly, repeating over and over what a fine scholar he was, and how brave, what a wonderful warrior, and how handsome too, and how much the people loved him.

Every word Doeg spoke fanned the King's anger until it began to smoulder, ready to burst into flame. He began to watch David closely, carefully. Was David really loyal to him? Or was not he secretly trying to overthrow him and become King before his time?

One day an unfortunate incident occurred. King Saul and his son Jonathan and his son-in-law David had been away at war with the Philistines. They returned victorious, and the women came dancing to greet them, playing music on the harp and cymbals. And to celebrate the victory, as they danced, they sang:

"Saul hath slain his thousands,
But David his ten thousands."

So! The people considered David a better warrior than King Saul!

The King brooded over this insult. He thought about it during the day, and those careless words of the dancing women kept sounding in his ears at night when he tried to sleep. His jealousy grew day by day, and he was less and less able to conceal it from his court, until soon it was an open secret.

Jonathan heard him murmur against David. Doeg heard him curse David. Abner heard him threaten David's life. And soon everyone knew that Saul hated David. Everyone knew that the King planned to kill David.

Everyone knew, except David himself, and when at last he heard it, he would not believe it. He dismissed it as idle court gossip. First his armor-bearer whispered it to him and David rebuked him and strode out to the pavilion to pace up and down, scoffing at the evil report. His wife Michal found him in the pavilion. She urged him to flee, to escape, warning him that Saul, her father, would surely slay him. He scolded Michal for repeating what he thought was stupid, idle gossip. And so he stalked away from her, out to the water gardens.

And there Jonathan found him.

"This is no idle gossip," Jonathan told him quietly. "It is the sad truth. My father, the King, plans to take your life. Flee, brother David, flee while there is yet time."

David believed Jonathan. His good friend Jonathan would always tell him the truth.

There was only one thing for him to do. He ran away.

First he fled to Ramah where Samuel, the Prophet, protected him. But word came that Saul was on his way to Ramah, to search him out and to run him through with a sword.

David escaped. He ran away to Nob. There the priests hid him away for a short time, until the news came that Saul was on the march again.

David fled from one refuge to another, from one hiding-place to another. Finally, exhausted, unable to run further, he reached the cave of Adullam which was deserted.

On hands and knees he crept into the cave, into the deepest corner, where he flung himself down and lay on his back, exhausted and ill. He could go no farther. He knew he could not hide there long. His old enemy, Doeg, had been spying on him all the way and now no doubt a messenger must already be hastening to Saul to report his whereabouts. So he was not safe here. But he was exhausted and here he would have to stay.

He lay flat on his back, resting. After a while, he sighed. He moved his right foot, ready to rise and resume his flight. But just then he felt something tickle the back of his hand.

He raised his hand and saw a little Spider crawling up his middle finger towards his knuckles. David smiled weakly, glad even for the company of a little Spider, providing it had not come to kill him too!

"Ho," he said. "Hello there, little Spider. What do you here?"

"Hello, David," squeaked the Spider in its threadlike voice. She moved her green and yellow-banded body to and fro on his hand as she spoke. "I come to keep you company, David, and to help you too."

David smiled wearily.

"For your company I thank you, Spider, for I am lonely indeed. But I am in great trouble. I am in very great trouble. What good could you possibly be? I am afraid you are useless to me. In fact," he continued, "I do not know what use you are to anybody. I wonder why God bothered to make so useless a creature as a Spider. All you can do is to spin a web. And what good is that?"

For a moment the Spider was quiet and still.

Then suddenly, furiously, she began to weave.

"Excuse my weaving," she squeaked. "But whenever I get excited I just weave and weave. O David, that was such a cruel thing to say!"

"Oh, I'm sorry, Spider. I didn't mean to hurt your feelings, but . . ."

"But." The Spider picked it up, without stopping her weaving. "Well, let me tell you one thing, my dear David. *Nothing* that God created is useless. *Everything* has its purpose."

"Yes, I know," David said wearily, truly sorry to have offended the Spider, but more sorry for himself. "I know everything on earth has a meaning. And I know that everything on earth was created for a purpose. And I supose, dear Spider, that there is some rhyme or reason in your spinning endless and countless webs. Though I confess, I can't see what that reason is."

"You don't have to know everything," the Spider squeaked angrily. "Just put your trust in God and the purpose of everything will come clear in time. Now, you don't suppose I just happen to be here by accident, do you?"

"Aren't you?"

The Spider laughed a squeaky, spidery laugh.

"Oh no," said she. "Not by accident. God sent me here to help you. And help you I will. You shall see."

David sighed and said nothing. But he thought, and his thoughts were hopeless and bitter. The Lord knows that I need great help and all He sends is this little Spider, I guess He doesn't really care about saving me or He would send hailstorms to rust Saul's sword or lightning to strike him blind. Oh no, the Lord doesn't care about saving me.

The Spider broke into his thoughts.

"Here you are, David." She handed him something. "Here's the little web I

began to weave when you made me so angry. You may amuse yourself with this little web while you sit and wait."

"No, no." David started to sit up.

The Spider tried to stop him, but of course, what could a Spider do against a strong man like David? He didn't even feel her pushing him back.

"No," he repeated. "I must not rest any longer. King Saul will be here soon. I must flee. I must find somewhere else to hide."

"Please lie down and rest, David," begged the Spider. "I told you I would help you and I will, when the time comes. Now listen to me. I know that a spy of Doeg's has gone to tell King Saul that you are here in the cave of Adullam."

"You see!" David cried, and started to get up.

"But you must not leave this cave, David," the Spider insisted. "They are on the way here. They will catch you on the road. Please lie back and rest and I shall tell you what I shall do."

She whispered in his ear.

He shrugged his shoulders and lay down again on the ground. He couldn't see how her scheme could help him but he was so completely exhausted, he could not

move on. Saul would catch him eventually. He might just as well catch him here.

Suddenly the Spider jumped on David's hand. And he jumped up. They both heard the same thing.

They heard the sound of trumpets. They heard the roll of drums, and then the clank of armor.

"King Saul!" whispered David. "He is near at hand!"

"Yes," the Spider whispered back as though there were anyone else to hear. "I haven't a moment to lose. I have to get busy. But just you rest yourself, dear David."

She crawled down his hand and across to the opening of the cave. And then, as David watched, she began to weave a web across the opening of the cave.

Against his will, fascinated by the furious industry of the Spider, David watched her work. And he discovered that weaving a web was not as simple a matter as he had supposed. The Spider was using great skill and David half forgot his worries while he watched.

The Spider was spinning an orb web, one made like a wheel, with spokes going from a center to the outer rim, the edges of the entrance to the cave. She finished two sides of the triangular frame and started the third side. She climbed back up the perpendicular line she had spun, reeling out a new line which she anchored at the base. Then she slung herself underneath the silky thread until she reached the end, then pulled in the slack that she had been carrying. She fastened it with a spot of sticky stuff that was like glue.

David watched, fascinated. Then, a sound outside awakened him again to his danger. The sound of the trumpets was coming nearer, nearer, too near, too close.

And the Spider worked fast, faster, faster, putting in the final lines as the sound of the bugles and the drums came closer and closer. And then, just when it seemed as if they were right outside the cave, she filled in the last radius. Then she rushed back into the cave and crawled up again on David's hand.

"You worked hard, dear Spider," David said. "It is a beautiful web, but useless, useless."

"Sh!" she whispered. "My work is finished. Your task, O David, is to be very quiet and to wait patiently."

David crouched at the opening of the cave in the shadows, the Spider resting motionless on his hand. She looked anxiously at the perfect orb web, hoping it would do the work for which it was intended. He looked at the web too, knowing now that it was a work of art, but still how weak and how puny it was to save a man from the wrath and the madness of a King.

"Halt!" came a shouted command from outside.

The Spider and the man heard the tramping, one, two, halt, as thousands of feet came to a stop. The drums rolled once more. The horns blasted the stillness. The trumpets announced the arrival of the King.

Then clearly they heard the voice of Saul, King of Israel.

He was standing directly in front of the cave, looking at the delicate and gossamer-like spider web hanging across the opening. King Saul shouted angrily,

"What false report was brought to me?"

Doeg came running forward. "No false report, Your Majesty. David *is* here, in the cave of Adullam. My spy has so reported."

"Your spy!" King Saul spat out scornfully. "What a stupid fellow he must be. Order him imprisoned."

"But Your Majesty," Doeg protested. "Why punish my spy? He brought no false report. David is hiding in this cave. I shall go in and drag him out."

"Wait!" the king ordered angrily. "David is not in this cave. He could not be. Look at that spider web."

"I see the spider web," Doeg said. "But what of it? It does not mean that David is gone from here."

"Oh yes, it does," the king shouted. "See how delicate that spider web is. If David had gone into that cave, he would have torn the web to shreds. That web must have taken hours to weave and David was seen on the road just a half hour ago. I tell you, David is not here. You are wasting time while David escapes. Let us hurry on."

"Just let me tear the web aside," Doeg begged. "Let me go in and prove that David sulks here in this cave!"

"No!" the King shouted in his rage. "No, I tell you. We have no time to lose. David is not there or the web would be shattered. Back! Back to Gilgal! We march back to Gilgal!"

Before Doeg could utter another protest, the King and the army, the trumpets and the drums, everything and everyone had turned around to march back to Gilgal.

Inside the cave, David was patting the little Spider's head.

"O little Spider, O clever little Spider," he said. "Never again will I say that anything that God created is useless. Everything has its purpose. Everything has its meaning. Today you spun a web across the rock. Today you saved my life. And I thank you, little Spider, I thank you."

The little Spider quivered and squeaked, and in her excitement she began to spin and spin, and to weave and to weave, another web, another web, to show her joy over having saved Israel's future King.

The Madman of Gath

When David first fled from the madness of King Saul, he hid in the cave of Adullam. Too wearied to run further, he had waited for Saul to capture him. But along came a Spider to spin a web across the rock which fooled the King into believing that David could not possibly be hiding in the cave.

And so the humble little Spider saved the life of David, the man who had killed the giant Goliath.

When the last roll of the drums and the sound of the marching of King Saul's army faded away, the Spider looked up at David.

"Where will you go now, David?" she squeaked.

"Where, indeed!" he answered gloomily. "I do not know where, friend Spider. But I shall keep on running away until perhaps one day King Saul will stop hating me. Then I shall return to my home and to my wife."

"God's blessing on you, dear David," the Spider said, picking her way along the Web. "I hope you will always escape from any danger you meet."

"Thank you, little Spider, for saving my life," David said. "And now, good-bye."

"Good-bye, David," she squeaked. "Good-bye."

David marched away from the cave of Adullam, over the stones and rocks. He struck off in the opposite direction to that which King Saul's army had taken. And hour after hour, he forced his way through thickets and across streams. Nightfall found him in a desolate, lonely spot, but he did not dare lie down to sleep in the open.

He knew that his enemy, the cunning Doeg, would not give up so easily. His spies at that very moment must be searching the whole countryside. So David pushed forward, stumbling against bruising rocks, finding a path through the forest, only to lose it again.

But still he struggled onward and all through the night he wandered. The first rays of the dawn found him at the edge of the forest, still on his feet, but staggering with fatigue. He sagged against a tree, his head hanging, his eyes closed.

Somewhere nearby, he heard the rumbling of a cart. He raised his heavy head and opened his tired eyes. And there, before him, stretched a city!

"A city!" he exclaimed. "The City of Nob! The City of Priests!"

He staggered forward on feet so swollen and bruised he would have fallen, but the hope of a refuge gave him enough strength to struggle to the gates of the city.

There he collapsed. But he roused himself enough to crawl inside the gates. And then he fell flat on the ground.

Nearby strolled a priest who saw the weary, dust-covered man fall. The priest hurried over to him, leaned down to look at his face, and exclaimed,

"David! It is David, the giant-killer."

David opened his eyes, and smiled weakly. He gasped,

"Water. Please, water."

"Lie quietly." The priest rose to his feet. "I shall get help."

He rushed away. David closed his eyes. A few moments later the priest came hurrying back with two young priests. The first one held a flask of water to David's mouth, and David drank, long and deeply. When at last he lifted his head from the empty flask, he said weakly,

"I thank you. You have restored my soul."

"Come," said the priest. "We shall help you to the Sanctuary. There you will find food and shelter."

The two young priests helped David rise from the ground. Then, their arms around his waist, his arms around their shoulders, they supported him all the way to the Sanctuary.

At its door stood the High Priest, Ahimelech.

"David!" he exclaimed. "You look exhausted. But we shall soon remedy that. We shall give you a bed to rest on and food to eat."

He turned and led the way. David, leaning on the two young priests, followed Ahimelech into the Sanctuary to a bedchamber. The priests gave him clean clothing to wear while his were being washed. Ahimelech himself brought him holy bread from the altar. And after he had eaten, they left him alone to rest.

The moment his head touched the pillow, he fell sound asleep. And he slept deeply for half the day. When he awakened, he put on his clothes which had been cleaned for him. Then he was ready to talk to Ahimelech.

He looked for him behind the Sanctuary and came upon him in the water-gardens. These four gardens were irrigated by intersecting trenches. At two of the gardens, two men were regulating the water into the trenches with short-handled hoes. And at the other two gardens, two men were regulating the water with their naked feet.

David stopped to look at them. One of the men acted strangely, flopping about as if he had no control of his muscles. Then he would dance a few steps, laughing wildly meanwhile. Then he grinned foolishly as he dug his big toe into the moist ground.

"The fool," David muttered. "The poor lunatic. It's always been a mystery to me, and haven't you wondered, Ahimelech? Why did God create lunatics? They're of no use to themselves or to anyone else."

"Perhaps there is a use for them," Ahimelech said quietly. "I can't answer your question but I am sure God has a purpose even for a lunatic. We don't know the reason, but there must be one."

"I can't see any good reason for lunatics." David brushed Ahimelech's arguments aside impatiently.

"There might come a time when you may beg to be mistaken for a lunatic," Ahimelech said quietly.

"Never!" declared David. Then he laughed. "But why should I spend precious time talking about lunatics. I must make plans for my safety. King Saul pursues me to the death."

"So I have heard," Ahimelech said. "What has happened?"

"The King is a very sick man," David said. "In his sick mind his love for me turned to hate, and I have had to flee."

"But you vanquished Goliath," objected Ahimelech. "You married Saul's daughter Michal. You helped him fight the Philistines. Would he really do you harm?"

"Aye," David said gloomily. "His mind is sick, and he does not understand, and I have had to flee."

A priest came running from the Sanctuary, calling,

"Ahimelech! King Saul's army advances on the City of Nob!"

"King Saul!" cried David. "He is coming for me."

"Remain here, David," Ahimelech said. "We shall protect you."

"No, no," David said. "If you protect me, Saul will destroy the City of Nob. He will slay all the priests and ruin the Sanctuary. I cannot stay and face his madness and his hatred. I must flee again. Good-bye, Ahimelech, good-bye. And thank you, thank you, good friend, for all your help."

He rushed out through the gates of the City of Nob. And now as he speeded along, he decided to run away to Achish. Although Achish was the King of the Philistines, he had become a friend of David's after the death of Goliath when the war quieted down. Surely he would offer his protection. Saul would not pursue him into the city of Gath. Perhaps there he could be safe.

His journey lasted for several days over the rough mountains and through thick forests of cedar trees until finally he stood outside the walls of Gath. He stopped there to rest. But he could not present himself at the court of Achish as he was, dusty and travel-stained.

So first he found a little brook with fresh, clear water. With a flat rock he beat the dust of the road out of his garments. With a handful of oak leaves he rubbed the mud of rivers from his sandals. Then he washed himself with cool water from the brook.

Now, although his clothes were ragged and his sandals were worn out, at least he was clean. He felt less like a fugitive and more like the son-in-law of Saul, King of all Israel.

Confidently he strode through the streets and up to the palace gates. These gates were guarded by two giants. Their names were Lahmi and Ishbi.

"Halt!" bellowed Lahmi.

"Halt!" boomed Ishbi.

David halted. He looked from one giant to the other. He said loudly,

"Present me to the King. Take me to Achish."

"Ho, ho!" Lahmi put his fists to his hips, threw back his head, and laughed. "Ho, ho, brother Ishbi, look who commands us."

"A little pigmy, and he gives us orders." Ishbi laughed too.

"Cease this foolish noise," David said. "I am David, the son of Jesse, of the land of Israel. Go, tell your King I await."

The two giants stopped laughing.

"Oh," Lahmi said slowly. "You are David, the son of Jesse."

"Oh," Ishbi said quietly. "You are David, from the land of Israel."

The two giants looked at each and nodded slowly.

David said, "Yes, I am David."

Then Ishbi said, "Indeed, we are glad to welcome you." He and Lahmi grinned at each other. "Very glad indeed. Come, David, son of Jesse. Come, David, of the land of Israel. Come with us."

Ishbi began to walk through the courtyard to the palace, and David followed him. Lahmi walked behind him. This single-file procession moved through the courtyard to the doors of the palace where a guard, on seeing the giants, threw wide the door. Then the procession moved onward, through halls made of marble.

Shrill, cackling noises echoed through the corridors. David, raising his head to listen, said,

"What noise is that? Who shrieks like that?

"The Queen and the Princess," Lahmi answered.

"The Queen and the Princess!" David exclaimed. "Why do they shriek so?"

Ishbi said, "They are sick. They are mad. They are insane."

"Insane," David murmured. "From one madness to another do I flee."

By now they had reached the audience chamber. The guard at the door opened it when he saw Ishbi, and Ishbi and David and Lahmi marched through the door and then stopped. King Achish was on his throne, alone in the audience chamber. He sat with his hand on his chin, looking into space, worrying about his troubles. Now, hearing footsteps, he raised his head.

"Whom bring ye here in my time of trouble?" he asked sternly. "I wish to see no one."

David rushed forward, away from the giants.

"I am David," he said. "David, the son of Jesse, of the land of Israel."

"Ah, David." King Achish smiled weakly. "David, my friend. It is good to see you. But I did not recognize you. Your clothing is torn and ragged."

David bowed before Achish.

"Ah, Your Majesty," he said softly. "I beg you to forgive my appearance. I am now a fugitive and a wanderer. I have been fleeing the wrath of a madman."

Achish frowned at the word 'madman,' but David did not notice. He went on,

"My father-in-law, Saul, the King of Israel, is sick in his mind. And he has turned to hating me. He pursues me with his army. He threatens me with death."

"You, David?" King Achish shook his head. "Saul pursues you? Ah, that is sad, sad, yes, sad indeed."

"I throw myself upon your mercy, Your Higness," David said. "Please give me shelter. Let me hide away here with you until King Saul shall have recovered his senses and no longer hates me. I shall repay you with loyalty and friendship."

"Welcome, David," the King said. "Here you are welcome. Here you may stay. I shall guard you and keep you from harm."

Achish sent servants scurrying for hot water and scented oils and clean clothing. After David had changed into the clean white clothing, he joined Achish in the grape arbor. The sun spotted through the leaves and birds sang high up in the branches, and for a moment the scene was quiet and peaceful.

But only for a moment.

Suddenly David was seized by the giant Lahmi, while Ishbi, the other giant, lunged at him with a sword. King Achish leaped to his feet and knocked Ishbi's sword out of his hand. Ishbi rubbed his wrenched wrist, looking sullenly at the King.

"Release my guest," the King ordered Lahmi.

Lahmi let go of David and moved to stand next to Ishbi.

The King frowned and said angrily, "Is this the way you treat the friend of the King?"

"He is our enemy," Lahmi muttered.

"He is our foe," Ishbi snarled.

"Your enemy?" David stared at the giants. "I have never harmed you. I have never seen you before."

"You have harmed us indeed," Lahmi growled. "We are the brothers of Goliath."

"Of Goliath whom you killed," Ishbi said.

King Achish moved to stand between his bodyguards and David, protecting David with his own body, facing the brothers. He spoke to them.

"It is true that David killed Goliath, but not out of hatred. Goliath challenged the armies of King Saul and insisted on the battle and David was forced to defend his King and his people."

One of the brothers smiled slyly and said,

"If that is the case, Your Highness, your throne belongs to David. For David defeated your champion. And to the victor belong the spoils!"

"That's why he has come," Ishbi shouted. "To take your throne."

Achish turned around slowly to look at David. David saw sudden doubt and suspicion on the face of the King. He sensed his danger. How to save himself! And then, in a flash, he knew what to do. He remembered the workman in the water-garden behind the Sanctuary at Nob.

He threw back his head and began to laugh, slowly at first, then more and more wildly, until finally he was screaming.

"Oho! Aha!" he laughed. "Aha! Oho!"

His crazy laughter mingled with the insane shrieking of Achish's wife and daughter echoing down the marble corridors.

"Oho! Aha!" David laughed. "Aha! Oho!"

Then he stood on his toes and began to spin around, like a top, faster and faster, laughing all the while, flinging his arms around. He stopped spinning and stopped laughing and dropped to his hands and knees, growling. He growled like a dog, then the growls grew louder until they sounded like the roaring of a lion. He threw himself flat on the floor, on his back, kicking his heels in the air, screaming a mumble-jumble of words that didn't make sense. Then suddenly he leaped up into the air and began to dance all around Achish.

The King backed away, shuddering. He scowled.

"What is this?" he shouted. "Is this another madman?"

Ishbi and Lahmi began to move away from David too, away from his swinging arms, away from his crazy laughter which was starting again.

"Is this man insane?" Achish demanded. "Don't I have enough lunatics in my house? Do I need another madman?"

David stopped laughing and made his eyes vacant. Then he began to advance on Achish, coming closer and closer. And Achish moved back and away from David, shouting to his bodyguards. "You are fools. He is just a luntaic. Away with him! Escort him to the borders of my kingdom. Let the poor crazy fool wander over the face of the world."

Achish rushed away, and the bodyguards grabbed hold of David by the arms, and dragged him along, through the court, out through the gardens, to the very borders of Gath. And there they flung him into the road. Ishbi and Lahmi turned back, wiping off their hands, as they went back to the Court of Achish.

David lay on the ground watching them go. He lay alone in the dust, and then a great calmness came over him. A song rose in his heart and these words came to his lips as he sang them:

> *"I will bless the Lord at all times;*
> *His praise shall continually be in my mouth.*
> *The Lord redeemeth the soul of His servants;*
> *And none of them that take refuge in Him shall be desolate."*

David rose from the earth, dusted off his clothes, and resumed his journey.

Abner and the Wasp

Abner was a great warrior, one of the heroes of King Saul's court. He was also in other ways a remarkable person. He was the son of the Witch of Endor and from her he learned many of the secrets of witchcraft. In addition, he was remarkable because of his astonishing size. Actually he needed very little help from his witch-mother because he was so tremendous a giant that his size and strength alone got him anything he wished. And he was proud of his strength. He was proud of being a giant and frequently he made this boast:

"If only I could catch hold of the earth at some point, I should be able to shake it!"

This proud, powerful warrior had great influence over King Saul and played an important part in King Saul's feud against David. He was not a bitter enemy of David's, as Doeg was, but through his pride in his strength he was responsible for many of David's misfortunes.

The time came when David, sick at heart with all this useless fighting, was eager to bring the quarrel to an end. King Saul on his part was equally tired of the struggle. More and more was he lonely for David, and he let word get out that perhaps he would welcome David back to his court, perhaps they could be friends again.

One of David's spies brought him this news.

"O David, all that the King wishes is that you should send him some proof that you too wish to make peace with him."

"Proof!" David cried. "I shall send the King proof of my good intentions, and speedily."

David's opportunity presented itself the very next day. His spies reported to him that King Saul would soon be travelling through the forest next to which David's camp was located. David disguised himself as a common soldier, covered his face and head with green leaves sewed together to make him look like part of the foliage, and hid himself behind some thick thorn bushes.

He crouched there for two hours, waiting for the King to pass those bushes. His back and legs were getting stiff from this crouching position. His eyes were smarting from staring at the path. Finally, deciding that the King wasn't coming after all, David was just about to sneak away back to his own camp, when, suddenly, he heard the sound of voices.

He waited motionless. As the voices came closer, he recognized them as King Saul's and Abner's and Doeg's. In front of them were four soldiers. They stamped past David's hiding place, marching single file. Then came Doeg, then the King, with Abner behind him.

"Let us pause for a moment to rest," King Saul said.

And he stopped right in front of the bushes where David was concealed!

"This is my chance," whispered David.

He took from his belt a long, sharp, pointed knife. Now he held the King's life in his hand. One quick thrust of this pointed knife into the back of the King, and Saul would be dead! David gripped the knife hard in his hand, leaned forward cautiously, but he did *not* trust the knife into the King's back. Instead, he caught hold of the King's long cloak without tugging at it, and, with the sharp edge of the knife, he cut off a small corner of it.

He moved back, stuck his knife into his belt, put the little fragment of the King's cloak into his pouch. Then on tiptoe, scarcely making a sound as he parted the branches of the bushes, he crept away from his hiding place, back to his own camp.

He summoned his most trusted scout, gave him the piece of cloth he had cut from the King's cloak, told him to run speedily to the King's camp on the other side of the forest with a message for the King.

The scout took a shortcut through the underbrush. He dodged from bush to tree and from tree to bush, and no one caught sight or sound of him. He emerged from the forest, reached the camp of King Saul safely and then purposely made a noise and showed himself, and let himself be captured by a sentry who stood on the outskirts of the camp. The sentry was going to march him off to the captain of the guards, when along came Abner. The scout recognized Abner and told him that he had a message for King Saul from David.

"For the King himself?" Abner asked.

"Yes, for the King himself."

"Then come with me."

Abner marched the scout to the King's tent.

King Saul was resting, musing over the quarrel with David, wondering why he had had no word from him when he had promised to send proof that he wished to make peace. Just then Abner strode into the tent with David's scout.

"Your Majesty," Abner said. "Here is a spy who claims to come from David."

"From David!" King Saul sat up straight. "Truly, do you come from David?"

"Yes, Your Majesty," the scout said, bowing to the King. "Truly I come from David. He has sent me to tell you that he wishes only peace with Your Majesty."

"What proof does he send?" King Saul asked eagerly.

"Before presenting the proof," the scout said, "I must tell Your Majesty how the proof came to be in David's possession."

"Speak! Speak!" King Saul commanded impatiently.

"An hour ago Your Majesty was walking through the nearby forest with your two lieutenants, Abner and Doeg. Is that not true?"

The King and Abner exchanged a quick look, each wondering how this scout could know that.

"Perhaps," the King said cautiously. "Perhaps."

The scout continued. "Your Majesty paused for a moment to rest next to some thorn bushes."

"Yes, yes," the King said, motioning him to speak on.

"Behind those thorn bushes," the scout said. "David was concealed, waiting. In his hand he held a long, pointed and very sharp knife. When Your Majesty paused next to those bushes, it would have been a matter of seconds for David to have stabbed you in the back."

"What a narrow escape!" Abner exclaimed.

"No, it was no narrow escape," the scout said, shaking his head. "The King was in no danger. David has never wished to take the life of the King. His Majesty was perfectly safe standing with his back to David even though David had a knife in his hand."

"Indeed, indeed," the King said wonderingly, rubbing his chin. "Indeed. David could have killed me in that moment. And he did not. Perhaps indeed David does wish to establish peace between him and me."

Abner moved impatiently.

The scout continued. "Your Majesty, David used that opportunity to cut this small piece of cloth from the bottom of your cloak."

He took the scrap of material out of his pouch and handed it to the King.

"A fragment of my cloak!" the King exclaimed. He shouted to an aide, standing nearby. "Run. Fetch the cloak I wore in the forest."

"Would you call this proof?" Abner said scornfully.

"Proof it is," the scout said. "David stood so close to the King, he could have killed him. But all he did was to cut off a corner of his mantle. Does that not prove David's great desire for peace?"

The aide came running with the King's cloak. He held it up and everyone present could see that a corner of the cloak was missing. The King fitted the fragment to the ragged edge of the corner. And it fitted!

"Yes, yes," the King cried. "This does fit the jagged piece of the cloak."

"I agree it fits," Abner said. "But even so, Your Majesty, that is no proof of David's friendship. I don't believe he was near those thorn bushes at all. This is what must have happened. Today when you walked in the forest, you must have caught your cloak on a thorn bush and a thorn tore your cloak, pulling off that piece of cloth. Later David happened to find it hanging on the bush and thought he could buy peace with this ragged cloth."

In bewilderment the King looked from Abner to his cloak to the scout. Then Abner's poisonous words took effect in his sick mind. And suddenly he roared at the scout,

"Scoundrel! Get you back to David. Tell him Saul is not to be captured with cheap tricks."

"It is no trick, Your Majesty . . ." the scout tried to insist.

But Abner rushed him out of the King's tent and out of the camp. There was nothing for him to do but to return and report failure to David.

David was downcast at this failure. He rewarded the scout for risking his life, dismissed him, and then sat for long hours trying to think of some plan which could prove to Saul that he was the King's friend. He plucked a few chords on his zither, letting the music soothe him. But that did not help for long, and hour after hour he brooded, dejected and disappointed.

When night began to fall, suddenly a plan sprang into David's mind. It would need secrecy to carry it out, so he settled himself in patience to wait for the night to come with its concealing blackness.

He sat at the door of his tent, his fingers softly plucking the strings of his harp, his eyes staring at the heavens. He waited for one star to appear, and another and another, until the heavens were filled with the stars of night.

He hung up his harp, stole quietly out of his tent and away from his camp, telling no one of his plan. Softly he crept through the forest until he reached King Saul's camp. He stopped at the edge of the forest, concealed himself behind the thick, round trunk of a tree, listening, waiting.

The night was black. The camp was still. There was no sound of voices. Everyone seemed asleep, except for the sentries. But still he waited, a few more minutes, another few, and then he crept forward out of the forest, into the clearing. He kept in the shadows, stealing past the first three tents until he reached the largest tent which he knew must be the King's. There he paused, waiting for the sentry stationed before the King's tent to march on his beat to the far corner.

When the sentry's back was turned, David crept forward noiselessly into the tent.

He stood motionless for a few moments to let his eyes become accustomed to the gloom. Finally in the far corner he could see Saul, sleeping peacefully, an aide lying on the floor at the left of his cot, his armor bearer lying on the floor on the right of his cot.

Inside of the door of the tent Abner was lying, sound asleep.

Now, thought David, if I really were the King's enemy, I could creep forward, kill him as he sleeps and steal out again with no one the wiser.

But since he had not come to kill the King, he turned his attention back to Abner who was stretched out across the whole front of the tent. He was so huge, he took up as much space as two men might have taken. He was sleeping on his back with his legs drawn up, and by his right knee there was a tall pitcher of water.

Ah, David thought, that could be my proof. If I could steal that pitcher of water...

He crept forward slowly, quietly, then dropped to his hands and knees to crawl on all fours. Soundlessly he moved forward inch by inch, listening to the heavy breathing of the sleeping Abner. David moved forward until he came to Abner's feet. Then he began crawling between Abner's legs until he reached the pitcher of water. He put his hand on it, lifted it and turned to crawl back out of the tent.

At that moment, Abner, in his sleep, brought his knees down and together. And David was imprisoned between those giant legs as if caught in a trap!

He was afraid to move. If he woke him up, Abner would kill him on the spot. If he did not waken Abner, he would be crushed between those powerful knees which were drawing closer and closer together. Already David could feel his breath coming faster. Already the blood was beginning to pound in his ears.

He prayed, oh he prayed quickly and mightily to the Lord to save him from being crushed between the knees of this giant! Those knees were pressing tighter and tighter...

Suddenly David heard a singing, a whispering, a buzzing sound which he thought must be in his own head as the life was being choked out of him. But the buzzing came closer and became louder and in the faint gloom David was able to see that it was a wasp circling his head, coming closer and closer.

The wasp had come to save him. It swooped down, away from David's head, down, down to Abner's knee. And right on the very kneecap, the wasp darted his stinger and gave Abner a mighty sting on the knee!

Abner cried out in his sleep and raised his knee. He did not awaken, but he spread his knees apart to get away from the pain, freeing David. And David backed out of the trap, took firm hold of the pitcher, crawled out of the tent, hurried along the shadows to the forest and escaped.

In the morning he sent another scout to King Saul with the pitcher of water. This scout went boldly to King Saul, placed the pitcher before him, bowed and said,

"O King, into your tent last night, David came stealing."

"What! Into my tent!" King Saul exclaimed. "He might have killed me!"

The scout nodded. "Your Majesty, that he might well have done. He had every chance. But he had not come to kill you. He had come to prove once more his friendship for you, and to show you that he had the chance to kill you, and did not; instead he stole this pitcher of water from between Abner's knees."

Abner laughed. "From between my knees! What nonsense. That pitcher of water. Do you call that proof? My servant must have lost it at the edge of the forest and David found it there."

"Yes, Abner," King Saul said glumly. "David must have found it in the forest."

"Of course, Your Majesty," Abner said. "Do you honestly think, O King, that that small David could have crept between my powerful, giant legs and not have been crushed to death?"

King Saul looked at Abner's powerful legs and shook his head.

"No, no," he sighed. "No man could have escaped being squeezed to death if caught between your legs, Abner. Send this spy back to David. Go, you wretch, and tell your master never to tell me lies again."

The scout hurried away.

And thus, because of Abner's false pride in his own strength, the feud continued between King Saul and David.

The Crumbling Walls

For the first time in many months, King Saul gave up his pursuit of David. He was battling the Philistines and for a brief period David felt secure. He was at his headquarters at Ziklag, walking in the garden with his captain Joab.

"This will not last, Joab," David said. "Saul will soon defeat the Philistines and then he will come hunting me again. Where will I go next?"

Joab said, "Oh David, why don't you put an end to this constant running away? Why don't you stay and do battle with Saul? You had it in your power to slay him many times. You could easily defeat him. Battle Saul, David. Defeat him. Then you will be King."

"Oh no." David shook his head. "I could never harm him. Saul was my friend. He was my king. No, Joab, indeed I have prayed to the Lord never to let Saul fall into my hands that I may never be tempted to kill him. No, Joab, let him live, and rule over Israel as King as long as he lives. There is time enough for me to be King."

Before Joab could answer, a soldier came marching up, leading a stranger whose clothes were dusty and torn as if he had been travelling a long time. He held something out of sight, hidden under his cloak. It made a big bulge.

The soldier saluted and said,

"O David, the sentry found this spy creeping into our camp."

"I am no spy," the man said.

"Who are you?" asked David.

"I am an Amalekite, my lord," the stranger said. "I come from Mount Gilboa where Saul has been fighting the Philistines."

"From Gilboa!" David exclaimed, grasping the man's arm. "Quickly. Tell me. How goes the battle? How fares my King, Saul?"

The man looked from David to Joab to the soldier, then to David again. He shrank back, trying to pull his arm out of David's grasp. But David held firmly, and Joab said,

"Speak up, man, speak up. How fares Saul, the King?"

The man lowered his head and said, "King Saul lies dead, and three of his sons."

"Dead!" cried David. "Saul is dead! And Jonathan?"

"And Jonathan," the Amalekite muttered.

"Oh, how are the mighty fallen," cried David.

> *"Saul and Jonathan,*
> *They were swifter than eagles,*
> *They were stronger than lions.*
> *How are the mighty fallen."*

The Amalekite stepped forward and from under his cloak brought forth the bulging object he had hidden there.

"O David," he said. "To you I have brought Saul's crown and his bracelet."

He handed the crown and the bracelet to Joab who turned to the sentry.

"Run," Joab said. "Call the wise Ahitophel."

And David said, "And let him summon the Sanhedrin. As for the Amalekite, bringer of evil news, away with him."

The sentry hurried the man away, and David and Joab went into the tent. David walked to the wall on which his harp hung, took down the harp and began to play, pouring out his sadness at the death of Saul and Jonathan, singing over and over,

> *"Saul and Jonathan,*
> *They were swifter than eagles,*
> *They were stronger than lions.*
> *How have the mighty fallen!"*

While he sang in praise of the dead, Joab went to the cedarwood chest from which he removed the Trumpets of Moses which had been fashioned in the desert

and had never been used since those ancient days. He placed the trumpets of Moses on a red velvet cloth, and next to it the crown and the bracelet of Saul.

Ahitophel came quickly into the tent. "Why have you summoned me? What has happened? Is anything wrong?"

David continued his mournful singing and did not answer. Joab stepped close to Ahitophel and whispered,

"The King is dead."

"Saul!" exclaimed Ahitophel. "King Saul is dead!"

"Saul is dead," repeated Joab. "Slain by the Philistines on Mount Gilboa. Saul and Jonathan both."

Ahitophel bowed his head. Joab whispered,

"David will be King, Ahitophel. Summon the Sanhedrin. Call the seventy men of the High Court of Israel to appear and witness the crowning of David as King."

Ahitophel nodded, and left the tent.

Before nightfall the assembly of seventy men crowded into David's camp.

Around them were grouped all of David's soldiers and all his faithful followers. In the very center of them all stood David, with Joab on his left side and Ahitophel, President of the Sanhedrin, in front of him. Ahitophel held Saul's crown and bracelet.

Joab held in his hands the Trumpets of Moses. He raised them to his lips and blew a clear, loud, piercing note. He blew another note, and a third. Then he lowered the trumpets.

A hush fell on the assembly. Ahitophel stepped forward and announced,

"I, Ahitophel, in the name of the Sanhedrin, proclaim a new King to rule over Israel. As Moses was the greatest of the prophets, so may David be the greatest of the kings. Hear me now, David, son of Jesse, I pronounce you King of Israel."

He raised the crown and placed it on David's head, while everyone cheered. David waited until the shouting died down, then he said in a clear, ringing voice,

"I was but a shepherd of flocks and a singer of songs. Now God has said to me: I take thee from following the sheep to be prince over My people Israel. Now that I am King, I shall keep watch over this people."

Feasting and celebration followed the coronation for several days. And then, when the noise of celebration died down, it was time for David to take up his duties as ruler of Israel.

The first task facing the new King was to conquer the city of Jerusalem which Saul had never taken from the Jebusites who lived there. David promoted Joab to be his general, and then they set their armies into motion. They marched on a hot, sunny day over the mountainous countryside until they reached the last hill in front of the city of Jerusalem.

From the hilltop they saw the mighty wall which protected the city. Onward they marched until they came to the north wall, to the grove of cypress trees, and here they pitched camp.

Before evening fell, one of the captains approached the King. He saluted David and said,

"Your Majesty, the sentry at the south wall reports that a Jebusite has been smuggled out of the gates. This Jebusite claims to have a message for your Majesty from the people of Jerusalem."

"Bring the man here," King David ordered.

A few minutes later the captain returned, marching his prisoner before him. The man bowed, and said,

"Your Majesty, I come from the people of Jerusalem with a protest. My people, the Jebusites, say that you have no right to attack them."

Joab laughed. "They complain? They protest? Isn't that laughable?"

But King David did not laugh. He silenced Joab and said to the Jebusite,

"State your complaint."

The man said, "If you attack Jerusalem, O King David, you will break an agreement made between our ancestors centuries ago."

"An agreement?" King David asked. "When did my people ever make an agreement with your people?"

The man turned towards the city walls and made a sweeping movement with his arm, pointing at the city.

"There in the city of Jerusalem," he said, "on that mountain top, stand two monuments of brass."

King David and Joab looked into the distance, at two objects which caught the gleam of the sun's rays.

"Those monuments of brass," the man continued, "stand as a reminder of the agreement. Many generations ago, your ancestor Abraham came as a stranger to our country and lived amongst the men of Heth who treated him as a friend. Came the day when Abraham's wife Sarah died and Abraham had no burial ground for her. He therefore bought the Cave of Machpelah from the men of Heth, but they made him promise that never would the people of Israel try to capture this city without the consent of its inhabitants. And, O King David, we do not consent!"

Joab shrugged his shoulders, then laughed. "Why must we be bound by an agreement which father Abraham made generations ago?"

The man pointed again towards the mountain inside the city.

"Those brass monuments," he said, "were erected by Abraham and the people of Heth to keep alive their agreement."

Joab would have answered again but King David signalled to the Captain.

"Keep this man under guard," he ordered, "until I have made my decision."

The captain marched the man away but they were hardly out of earshot when Joab said impatiently,

"What is there to decide? Abraham's agreement with the men of Heth does not concern us."

David shook his head. "Not so fast, my general. Not so fast. If Abraham made an agreement that the people of Israel must never conquer Jerusalem, we must go slowly. An agreement is not to be broken without just reason. We must decide whether we have the right to go contrary to father Abraham's word."

Joab moved impatiently, and David said,

"The Jebusites seem to have a strong case. We must not violate justice. This matter must be placed before the High Court. The Sanhedrin itself must decide whether we may attack Jerusalem or not."

King David thereupon prepared a statement addressed to Ahitophel, the President of the High Court. He sealed it in a pouch, and ordered one of his captains to go back to Gilgal and present it to the Sanhedrin. The captain left immediately, hurrying through the forests and across streams, stopping only to eat and rest, until he reached the Sanhedrin. He presented himself to Ahitophel and handed over the King's pouch.

Ahitophel broke the seal on the pouch, read David's message and immediately called a session of the High Court. When everyone was quiet and ready to listen, Ahitophel rose and read the King's statement.

> "To the honored members of the High Court:—
> I, King David, am encamped around the City of Jerusalem, but the Jebusites in the city have sent to inform me that long ago our father Abraham had made an agreement with the people of Heth never to capture the city. I now enquire of you:—
> Does that agreement still stand after so many generations?
> Signed:—David, King of Israel"

When Ahitophel finished reading, the seventy members of the High Court studied the case from every angle. Finally they pronounced their decision. Ahitophel wrote out the decision together with the reasons for it, sealed it in a pouch, gave it to the captain, who thanked Ahitophel and the High Court and left at once to return to David's camp.

The King and his general were waiting in the grove of cypress trees in front of the north wall. The captain saluted the King, presented the pouch to him and withdrew. King David broke the seal, pulled out the message and read aloud:—

> "O King David, be thou advised that upon due investigation the Sanhedrin has decided that the old agreement between our father Abraham and the people of Heth was broken long ago. The people of Heth have been gone for many, many years. The men of Jerusalem who defy you today are not the descendants of these men of Heth with whom the agreement was made. These are other heathens who took the city away long ago from the children of the friends of Abraham. Thus if you and your armies are now to storm the wall of Jerusalem and capture the city, you would not be breaking any agreement."

"Good!" exclaimed Joab.

"Wait," King David said. "There is more to the message."

> "But, O King, there is one warning we give. Before Jerusalem can be conquered, you must destroy the brass monuments which Abraham

and the men of Heth erected. As long as those monuments stand, you will never pass those walls. The strength of the walls is in the monuments."

"Fine," Joab said. "That is your answer, King David. The brass monuments will be easy to destroy. We are free to attack Jerusalem."

"But these high walls are impossible to climb and they are well guarded," King David said. "First we must find a way of getting into the city. Then we will worry about the brass monuments."

"I cannot understand what the monuments have to do with the walls," Joab said, "but if Ahitophel says we must destroy them first, I think I know how to do it. I have been studying these walls and I have a plan to get into the city."

He looked around at the grove of cypress trees and selected the tallest one. He ordered a soldier to climb up into the tree and bend down the tip of the tallest branch. The soldier climbed up the trunk, then into the branches until he reached the highest of them. He crawled out onto the branch and the weight of his body began to bend the branch towards the ground until it tipped down low enough for Joab to grasp it.

"Now jump off," Joab ordered the soldier, holding firmly to the branch of the tree.

The soldier jumped off. When he was away from the tree, Joab took one jump which lifted him off the ground and, clinging tightly to the branuh, he sailed into the air as it rebounded—and dropped him right on top of the high wall!

He turned, waved goodbye to David and quietly slipped down the other side of the wall until he touched the ground. He hid there in some bushes until night came. Then cautiously he made his way through the city, covered by the darkness. No one saw him. He moved on and on until he reached the mountain which rose from the center of the city. He climbed up the mountain to the top where the two brass monuments stood.

He pulled a small ax out of his belt and began to chop at the monuments.

The moment Joab swung his ax, something remarkable began to happen. A cracking noise was heard near the top of the outer wall of the city and in a moment a huge rock on the top of the wall rolled off. Joab chopped again and another rock dropped from the wall. With each sliver of brass that Joab chopped off the monument, a rock fell off the wall, and, miraculously, the wall began to crumble near the top. Joab swung his arm again and the ax-blade bit into the brass of the monuments. And with a great crashing of rocks and splintering of stone, the wall crumbled still more and became lower and lower until finally it was only a mass of crumbled stone.

And David and his armies were able to march right over the broken rocks into the city!

The Jebusites were taken by surprise and were quickly overcome by David's mighty army. By that time, Joab had completed the destruction of the brass monuments and within a very short time the people of Israel were in control of the city.

Then David proclaimed Jerusalem to be the capital of his kingdom. And Jerusalem remained the capital as long as the kingdom endured.

Footsteps in the Branches

"Long live the King! Long live the King!"

Saul, the King of Israel, was dead. David, the son of Jesse, now ruled as King over all Israel. And the people shouted,

"Long live the King! Long live the King!"

These shouts, we are told, were gathered together on the wings of the Angel of the Winds who carried the words right up to heaven to the Throne of Glory. Seated around the Throne were the Archangels, Michael and Raphael and Gabriel. The Angel of the Wind released the words he carried on his wings and at once they talked up.

"Long live the King! Long live the King!"

The Angel of the Wind silenced them by covering them with his wing. And then he said,

"Know you what King these words proclaim?"

Michael laughed. "O Angel of the Wind! What a foolish question! Of course the Lord knows what King the words honor. Was it not the Lord Himself Who gathered the soul of Saul in death so that David might live as King?"

"But why?" the Angel of the Wind asked. "Saul was a good King. O Lord, why did You want David to rule instead?"

Quickly the Angel Chorus around the Throne sang, "Holy, Holy, Holy is the Lord of Hosts," to cover up what they thought was an impudent question.

But the Lord silenced them, and spoke.

"Saul was indeed a good King. He was a good servant unto Me. But at times he did lack faith in Me. Not so David. David always listens to Me and never disobeys. Watch, My angels. I shall give you proof of David's loyalty. Look you down into the Valley of the Giants."

The Angels looked through all the heavens down into the Valley of the Giants. There in Rephaim, the Philistines were encamped, prepared to wage war on David and the armies of Israel. King David's soldiers had pitched their tents at Baal-Perazim in a grove of mulberry trees. Now they were waiting for the signal that the battle was to begin.

The soldiers could see smoke rising from a shaded hill in the enemy's camp across the valley.

"Look at the heathens," sneered one soldier. "Worshipping their false idol."

"Aye, they worship a little statue called Moloch," said another soldier.

"Yes," said a third, "and to worship Moloch they bring human sacrifices."

"This would be a good time for us to attack them," said the first soldier. "While they are busy worshipping their false god, we could advance on them."

So too thought King David, sitting alone in his tent. This would indeed be a good time to attack the Philistines. But first, he said to himself, first he would consult God in prayer. So he sang a hymn to the Lord:

"Hear the right, O Lord, attend unto my cry;
Give ear unto my prayer from lips without deceit.
Let my judgment come forth from Thy presence."

He stopped his prayer and waited. Then he heard the voice of the Lord, saying,

"Speak, David. Speak, My son."

"O Lord," said David. "The Philistines are encamped against me. Shall I, O Lord, do battle with the Philistines?"

"Yes, David," said the Lord. "Do battle with the Philistines."

"But, O Lord," David asked. "If I go to war with them, will You grant me victory?"

"Fear not. I shall deliver the Philistines into thy hand."

"I thank Thee, Lord. I thank Thee," David said. "I go now into battle."

"No, David, no," came the voice of the Lord. " Not yet. The time is not now."

"But, O Lord," David said. "Now the Philistines are unprepared. They busy themselves with the worship of their heathen god Moloch."

"Have I not said that I will help you in this war with the Philistines?" asked the Lord. "But first I must punish their heathen gods."

"As you did with the Egyptians?" David asked.

"As I did with the Egyptians," said the Lord. "Before I destroyed the Egyptians who enslaved My people Israel, first I destroyed their gods. Before I now destroy the Philistines who war against My people Israel, first I shall destroy their gods."

"But how shall I know when their gods are destroyed and my armies may attack?" David asked.

"I shall give you a sign," said the Lord. "Wait and listen. Wait and see. Wait until you hear the sound of Angels marching in the tops of the mulberry trees."

The voice faded.

For a moment all was still. Then outside David's tent came the sound of many voices. The curtains of the tent parted and in came the King's armor-bearer.

"What is the sound of these voices?" David asked.

"It is the soldiers," the armor-bearer said.

"What is all this noise I hear?" the King asked.

And the armor-bearer answered, "The men surge forward to the tent of the King to beseech him to advance now upon the Philistines."

At that moment General Joab burst into the tent.

"The soldiers are impatient," he shouted. "They want to begin the battle. Let us attack, they shout. Let us attack now."

"I shall speak to them," David said, rising from his throne.

The armor-bearer picked up his trumpets and preceded Joab out of the tent. And David followed them. The armor-bearer raised the trumpets and blew a loud, piercing note. Instantly all the men crowding into the clearing before the King's tent fell silent.

King David raised his voice so all could hear. "Patience, men. The time to attack the Philistines is not now."

"It is! It is!" shouted one voice from out of the crowd.

"Silence!" thundered Joab.

"No, let them speak," King David said.

"Now is the time," the same voice shouted. "The Philistines are at worship before their idol. They are offering their human sacrifices. Now is the time to attack, O King."

King David raised his sword and held it high. The sun glistened on it. And all the men looked at it.

"Now is not the time," the King said. "It is I who shall give the word when the time has come."

The men fell back sullenly, but obediently. They formed themselves in their ranks at a command from Joab. And they waited, with King David mounted on his steed before them, his armor-bearer to one side, Joab on the other.

As the men stared across the valley, the flame from the Philistine altars began to die down, and then disappeared. In place of the flame came the gleam of shining armor. The Philistines were on the move. They were advancing into battle.

"They come!" a soldier shouted.

"The Philistines are on the march!" shouted another.

"Give us the order, O King," shouted a third."

"Give us the order to attack!"

But King David held his sword high again and shouted, "No! Now is not the time."

This time it was was Joab who contradicted him.

"But, Your Majesty, there is not much time left. The enemy moves towards us. Are we not even to defend ourselves?"

David answered loudly so that all could hear. "Listen to me, Joab. Listen to me, men of Israel. God has forbidden me to attack the Philistines until we see the tops of the mulberry trees begin to move. We must not disobey the Lord, or we shall die. Let us have confidence in God. We shall attack when the tops of the mulberry trees bend beneath the tread of Angels' feet."

"The mulberry trees?"

"Beneath the tread of Angels' feet?"

Every man turned away from watching the approaching Philistines. Now every eye was fixed on the tops of the mulberry trees. But the tree-tops were motionless. Not a breeze stirred to ruffle the smallest leaf. The trees stood steady. The tops of the trees were still.

And the Philistines came closer and closer.

And still the the tops of the mulberry trees did not move.

"We shall be massacred," Joab muttered.

"Patience," King David said. "Patience, Joab. The trees have not moved."

The Philistines moved closer and closer. And the winds were still and not a leaf rustled on the mulberry trees. The tops were motionless, and the Philistines came nearer and nearer.

"We shall be butchered to a man!" cried the armor-bearer.

"Have faith in the Lord," King David said calmly. "We wait until the tops of the mulberry trees move."

"But the Philistines come closer!" a soldier cried out.

"Wait! Wait!" shouted King David. "Wait for the Lord!"

And closer and closer, and nearer and nearer came the Philistines until the armies of Israel could see their swords glistening in the sun. And closer and closer they came until the armies of Israel could see the design engraved on their shields. And still the tops of the mulberry trees were motionless.

And closer and closer the Philistines came until only an arrow's flight separated them from the Israelites.

"Attack now!" shouted Joab. "Attack, or we are ruined!"

"No, no!" shouted King David.

"The trees!" shouted the armor-bearer. "Look at the trees. They move!"

Not a breeze stirred, but suddenly the tops of the mulberry trees began to sway and to move and to dance as the Angels came rushing along to help King David and his armies.

"Attack!" shouted King David. "The Lord fights with us! Attack!"

And the Israelites made a sudden and a violent attack on the armies of the Philistines.

It was a hard battle, even with the Angels of the Lord to help. And the battle raged long and fiercely. But slowly the Philistines began to fall back, and then more quickly, and then those who had not been slain in battle turned and ran. They ran from the armies of King David and the Angels of the Lord.

Up in heaven God said to the Angel of the Wind,

"You see, My Angel. Now you see that David always obeys Me. He always awaits My word. He waited, even in the face of certain death. It is for this faith and trust in Me that I set David as King of Israel over Saul."

"Now I see," said the Angel of the Wind.

And with that, he released the words he had been holding down with his wing. And the words sprang up and shouted,

"Long live the King! Long live King David!"

The Giant Slingshot

The Amalekites were a fierce, war-like people. They were constantly fighting the children of Israel. But when David became King, the people of Israel grew strong. The Amalekites began to hear wondrous stories of the courage and strength of King David. They heard fearsome tales about the hero of David's armies, the mighty general, Joab. And the Amalekites began to avoid battle with the forces of Israel.

Quietly they withdrew behind the fortress of Rabbah, their capital city.

One day, King David summoned his general, Joab, and said,

"The time has come to declare our nation at peace."

"Not yet, King David," Joab said. "We shall not live at peace until we have broken the power of the Amalekites. Give me permission, O King, to wage war against the Amalekites and I shall destroy this danger forever."

"I grant you permission, Joab," King David said.

And Joab and his army marched off towards Rabbah. When they reached the fortress city, for the first time Joab was not so certain of victory. At a glance he saw that the mighty walls of the fortress would not yield to attack. The Amalekites were secure against invasion behind their strong defenses.

Joab studied the walls for their weakest points. But the walls had no weak points. They were strong throughout. He disguised some of his men as Amalekites and sent them secretly over the wall. But they were trapped, and still Joab was on the oustide of the walls, seeking a way in.

For six long months he planned, without success. Finally the soldiers grew restless. They chose a captain of the guard to go to Joab and ask permission for them to go home. The captain of the guard went to Joab's tent and found the general working at a new plan to storm Rabbah.

"Sir," the captain said. "I come as the representative of the soldiers. They are all saying that Rabbah cannot be conquered. They wish to return to their homes and to their wives and to their children."

Joab looked up from his papers and smiled. He said,

"We must not retreat. If we raise this siege and return to our homes, the heathen Amalekites would call us cowards. No, this is no time for retreat."

"But," objected the captain. "If we remain here and make no progress against the Amalekites, they will mock us all the more."

"True," Joab said. "But there is still one more reason why we must not retreat. If we leave now, these Amalekites, thinking we are weak, will unite many heathen nations to war against us. Now, I have a new plan, a bold plan, but a good one. Come with me to the parade grounds."

The two men left the tent and on the way to the parade grounds, Joab unfolded his scheme. At first the captain was amazed at its boldness. Then he objected to it, fearful that it would fail. And then he begged Joab to discard the idea. But Joab only laughed.

When they reached the parade grounds, the captain summoned the soldiers. They came quickly, but, to their surprise, instead of making a speech thanking them for their loyalty and granting permission for them to break camp, Joab snapped out orders to three men.

"Armor-bearer!"

The armor-bearer stepped forward and saluted.

"Fetch me my special sword."

The armor-bearer saluted again and hurried away.

"Paymaster!"

The paymaster stepped forward and saluted.

"Bring me one thousand pieces of gold."

The paymaster saluted again and rushed off to the treasure tent.

"Sergeant-of-the-Stores."

The sergeant-of-the-stores stepped forward and saluted.

"Go," Joab ordered, "and bring me a large piece of canvas."

The sergeant-of-the-stores saluted and walked briskly away.

Joab turned to the soldiers, and now he spoke to them.

"Soon you will return to your homes. I am bidding you be patient for forty more days. I promise you this, that if I have not conquered Rabbah in forty days, you may return home."

Just then the armor-bearer, the paymaster and the sergeant-of-the-stores came runing back. The armor-bearer carried Joab's special sword. The paymaster clutched a bronze box containing one thousand pieces of gold. And the sergeant-of-the-stores lugged a huge piece of canvas.

Joab directed the palmaster to put the thousand pieces of gold into a heavy leather pouch. Then, at Joab's instructions, he fastened it to an iron chain and bound it around Joab's left wrist.

"Now my sword," Joab commanded.

The armor-bearer came forward and fastened the sword into the scabbard at Joab's waist.

Joab turned to face the army, and he said,

"Now listen carefully for you must take part in this. Before we can defeat the Amalekites, we must conquer this stubborn wall."

"But we cannot," objected one of the lieutenants.

Joab smiled. "Cannot? At last I think we can."

He pointed to the sergeant-of-the-stores who was holding the canvas, and said, "I shall lie down in this canvas as in a hammock. And four of the strongest soldiers will swing me to and fro and then *fling* me as from a giant slingshot over the wall into Rabbah."

"Fling you into the city?" his armor-bearer asked. "You will be dashed to pieces. Even if you land safely, the Amalekites will kill you."

But Joab said, "Fear not. I will land on my feet and conceal myself at onue. Now hear me further. After I am in Rabbah, you will wait forty days. At the end of that time, attack the city!"

He motioned to the sergeant-of-the-stores to stretch out the canvas on the ground. Joab set himself in the center of the canvas. He pointed to four soldiers.

"Grasp the canvas," he ordered.

The four soldiers, two at each end, grabbed hold, and began lifting it from the ground. They heaved, lifted their arms, straining with the weight. Once they swung the canvas, twice and three times, each time the swing increasing. At the fourth time, as the swing started upward, Joab shouted,

"Let go!"

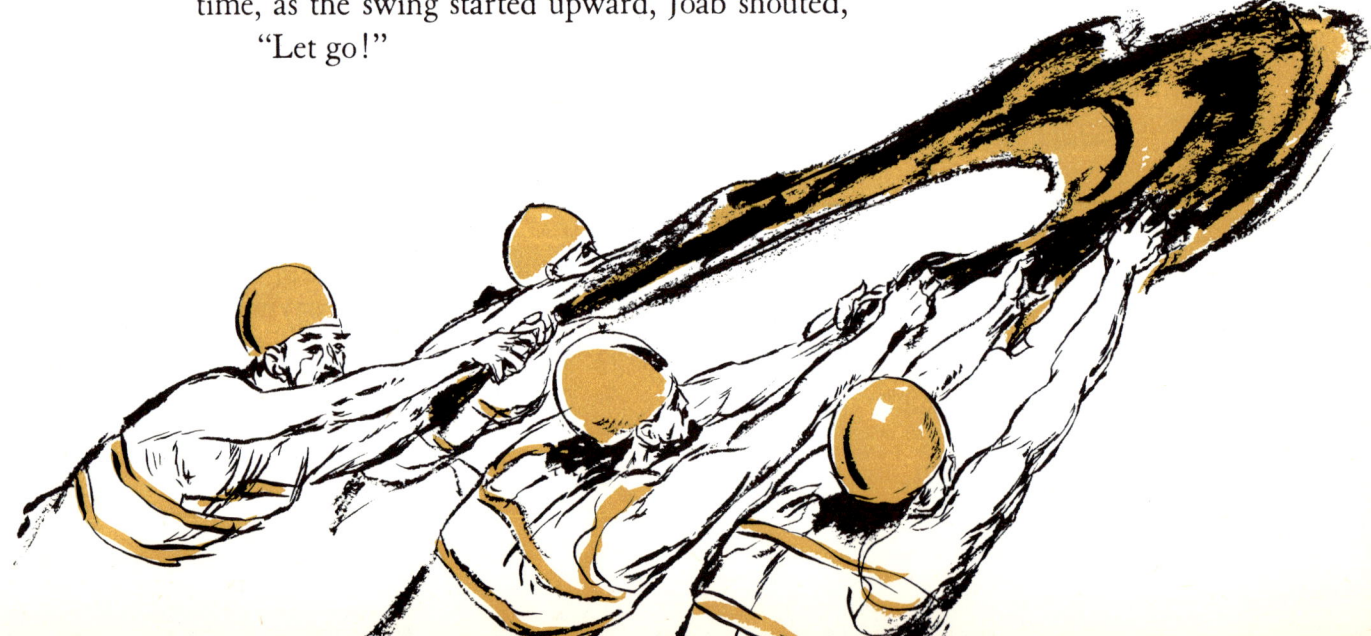

The soldiers released their hold, and the slingshot hurtled Joab high into the air. He went flying through the air and over the wall, his body twisting and turning, and then he fell down, down, down.

It was a long drop, but fortunately he landed in a pile of sand just inside the wall. He was dazed and hurt and for a while he lay still where he had fallen.

He had landed in the courtyard of a widow who had no warrior sons, only one daughter. The girl heard the crash and she came running out of the house. She gasped when she saw Joab, and then, seeing the blood streaming down his face from a cut on his forehead, she cried out and started to run to help him. But as she came closer and saw that he wore the clothes of an Israelite, she screamed and turned to run away.

Joab called after her. "Please, don't be afraid. I can't hurt you. You see I am wounded."

He groaned loudly, pretending to be hurt more than he actually was. At his first groan, the girl stopped running. She looked back at him over her shoulder. Then she tiptoed back and stared down at him. Joab groaned and moaned. Very weakly he said, gasping as if he had no breath,

"Take pity on me. Please. Lead me into your house. Oh, help me. I am dying."

He groaned again.

"Oh, you poor man," the girl said.

She helped him get to his feet and led him towards the house. He leaned heavily on her as though he could hardly walk. Inside the house, as she helped him sit down in a chair near the table, the widow came running in from another room. She screamed at her daughter, scolding her,

"He is our enemy. Do not bring him into the house!"

"Oh, my good lady," Joab gasped weakly. "I am no enemy. I am an Amalekite. I was caught behind the Israelite lines, and the only way I could escape was to change uniforms with a wounded warrior. In the dead of night I climbed over the wall and waited for daylight to get back into our own city. I had to jump from the top of the wall and I am hurt. Now I need help."

"I can't believe that story," the woman said.

Joab groaned, and the girl pleaded with her mother.

"Oh mother," she said. "Can't you see the poor man is hurt?"

Joab gasped, "Besides, I have money. I can pay my way."

"You have money?" the woman asked eagerly.

"Oh yes," Joab said quickly. "I have a great deal of money and I can pay for everything I need. And I'll pay you for your kindness too, if you will help me."

"Ah well," the woman said. "I would not turn a wounded man away from my door. We shall help you."

The woman, lured on by the gold in Joab's pouch, and the girl, stirred by sympathy, did everything they could for him. They fed him and doctored him and hid him so that no one would know he was there. They gave him a soft bed to sleep on, and bought new clothes for him. As soon as he put them on, his disguise was complete. Now he looked like an Amalekite.

Under the care and nursing of the widow and her daughter, and the good, rich food they fed him, he slowly regained his strength. But it took ten days for his wounds to heal, and then he was strong enough to go out into the city.

On the first day he walked round and round, amazed to find how large it was. He reconnoitered and spied out the spots in which he was interested. He located the palace in which Malcalm, the King dwelt. He found the various barracks where the soldiers were quartered.

On the second day, he went to an armorer. When he had fallen into the widow's courtyard, he had broken his sword. When he showed the armorer his sword, the man was amazed.

"I have never seen so wonderful a sword," he gasped.

"Repair it," Joab ordered.

"I cannot," the armorer said wonderingly, turning the sword over and over in his hands. "I have no materials that are as good or as strong. But I shall undertake, sir, to make you another. I shall make you a very strong sword. I shall have it for you tomorrow."

Joab returned the next day. With great pride the armorer handed him the new sword he had made during the night. Joab took it in his hand and snapped it in two.

The armorer was speechless.

"Do you call that a good sword?" Joab shouted. He flung the pieces on the floor. "I want a strong sword. I have gold. I have enough gold to pay for a good sword. Make me a strong sword, one I cannot break in two."

He strode out of the shop, leaving the armorer pale and trembling. He had never seen a man break a sword in two. So he doubled the amount of strong metals and spent the whole day over his anvil, beating out a good sword, a really strong sword.

And the next morning when Joab strode into the shop, the armorer confidently handed Joab the new sword. It was bigger and stronger than the first. Joab picked it up, looked it over critically. He held it between his hands, twisted his wrists, and with a turn of his fingers he bent the sword. It snapped in two. Again he threw the two pieces on the floor and now he shouted angrily at the man,

"This is a sword for a child. It breaks in my hand like clay. Make me a sword! A good sword! A strong sword!"

And again he strode out of the shop.

Now the poor armorer was terror-stricken. Who could this giant be? He could not be just an ordinary man. Oh surely he must be not a mere man at all but a demon. Perhaps, the man whispered to himself, perhaps it was Asmodeus, the King of the Demons?

Now the armorer was really frightened and he took three times the amount of bronze and other materials needed to make a strong sword. He worked all through the morning, hammering, cutting, shaping. And he worked all through the afternoon, and all through the evening and into the night, not sleeping, not eating, just hammering at the metal.

When the first streaks of the morning sun began to creep along the floor of the shop, the armorer, exhausted but triumphant, held in his hand the strongest sword that had ever been made in all of Rabbah.

A few minutes later Joab strode in and demanded his sword.

The armorer, smiling confidently, handed the new sword to Joab. He took it in his hand, felt its weight, and began to nod. Then he tried to bend the sword, twisting it, turning it, pressing all his weight on it, bending, turning, twisting, pulling. But he could not break the sword. The sword was strong. It was powerful.

The armorer relaxed and smiled. Joab smiled too, and took some gold pieces out of his pouch and paid the man.

Then he strode out of the shop, and down the road until he came to the first garrison of the king's soldiers. Without warning he attacked. He caught them unawares, and with his mighty sword he slew hundreds and hundreds of soldiers. Then he marched on to the next garrison to attack it. Before the guards knew what was happening, Joab with the mighty sword slew hundreds and hundreds of soldiers.

Then he went quietly, unnoticed, back to the house of the widow.

Throughout the city panic began to rage. People heard of the two garrisons which had been attacked by one man. The stories began to pile up and get bigger and bigger with each fanciful addition. It was a regiment of men, it was an army, it was . . . no, the stories finally boiled down again to one man. Then it must be the King of the Demons. Asmodeus was raging through the city! Asmodeus, the King of the Demons, would destroy every Amalekite in Rabbah!

They ran into their houses and bolted the doors and the windows. Every shutter was closed. Every gate was locked. The streets were empty. Not a single person was to be seen. For several days the Amalekites crouched behind their locked doors, not daring to budge, until finally, hunger began to drive them forth to the market. Hunger and the absence of news of any more killings. Little by little the people began to venture forth. And little by little life began to stir again in Rabbah.

When forty days had passed, the captain of the guards ordered the attack on the city.

Meanwhile inside the fortress, Joab mounted a high tower and in ringing tones shouted aloud so the whole city could hear:

"The Lord will not forsake His people!"

The Israelites, storming through the gates of the fortress, heard this booming voice shouting:

"The Lord will not forsake His people!"

And the Israelite soldiers streamed through the gates and assaulted the city, fighting fiercely. The terrified garrisons did not resist long, and thus Joab's army captured Rabbah. Joab, from his position on the high tower, watched the battle rage. When it ended, and victory was complete, he descended from the tower and, marching at the head of his army, went to the palace which was now unprotected. Joab marched into the throne room where Malcam, the King of the Amalekites, with the crown of pure gold on his head, sat on his throne. His warriors had fled and there was none to protect him.

Joab walked up to the throne. He stopped before the King. He saluted.

"Malcam, King of the Amalekites, your city has fallen and you are King no longer. Descend from your throne. We will bring you before King David."

Without a word, Malcam rose, descended from the throne, took off his golden crown, and said,

"Then give this golden crown to David, King of Israel, my master."

And Joab and the King, followed by the warriors of Israel, marched through the captured city, and turned their faces towards Jerusalem.

Sixty Breaths of Sleep

One fine autumn day, King David was hearing law-suits in his audience chamber. Court was in session, but the King was gazing out of the north window and seemed to be paying no attention to the proceedings. To one side of him sat his teachers and advisers, Ira the Jairite, and Mephibosheth. Mephibosheth was carefully following the testimony in each case brought before the court. But Ira watched the King as he stared out of the window.

During a lull in the proceedings of the court, Ira said to David,

"Your Majesty, I have watched you gazing out of the window. It is a perfect day for hunting. Perhaps you wish you were out in the forest, chasing a gazelle or a bear."

"Oh no," David answered. "I do wish I were doing something else, Ira, but not hunting. No, I wish I were studying. I wish I were writing a Psalm. There is so much writing and so much studying I must do, that sometimes I resent the time all these court matters take. I wish I could give all my time to the Psalms and the Torah."

"Study is good," Mephibosheth spoke up. "But first, O King, must come the business of life itself. As King you must govern your kingdom. You must direct your generals. You must decide cases of law when the people come before you for judgment. Then, in the time left over, you may devote yourself to your studies."

"But alas," King David complained. "There is no time left over. When I finish with all the business of my court, with all the affairs of my kingdom, there is only the night time left."

"And the night time must be used for sleep," Ira said. "Sleep is important too. You must rest the body and the mind, and sleep brings the best rest."

"Perhaps, perhaps," Mephibosheth argued. "But may I remind you of the time when Moses went up into heaven to receive and learn the Law? At that time God taught him his lessons at night because, said the Lord, the best time for study is in the stillness of the night hours."

"I'm glad to hear that," King David said. "I have always resented the hours I waste in sleeping. From now on I shall do my studying and writing during the quiet hours of the night."

"Bad solution," grumbled Ira. "I do not like that idea at all. When will you sleep?"

"Oh, I shall sleep for sixty breaths," King David said.

"Sixty breaths." Ira sighed. "That is not sufficient sleep. You know that. Besides, how will you know when to wake up? How will you know when the sixty breaths of sleep are finished?"

"The cock will crow," Mephibosheth said. "He will be awakened by the crowing of the cock."

"Now truly you are jesting," Ira said impatiently. "The cock crows at dawn..."

But Mephibosheth interrupted him. "Not the first time. Don't you know that famous legend, the one that tells how the rooster praises the Lord?"

"Everything praises God," Ira muttered, annoyed at having Mephibosheth tell him a legend he didn't know.

"No, no, don't be so cross," Mephibosheth said. "The tellers of tales recount a charming story. Listen, my friends:

> "Every night as the hour approaches midnight, the Lord visits the pious souls residing in Paradise. As soon as His Presence hovers over the pious, the Trees break out in song, to express their adoration.

The songs of the Trees awaken the Rooster. Thereupon he begins his praises of God. Seven times he crows, and at the seventh time he sings:

"'It is time to work for the Lord'."

"There's your answer, Ira," King David cried. "I shall sleep with one ear open, to hear the crowing of the cock. Then I shall know I have slept enough, and that will be my sixty breaths of sleep."

This conversation was interrupted by the calling of the next case. The session of the court resumed. Although David was still day-dreaming about the Psalms and the Torah and the rooster and sixty breaths of sleep, he was able to decide every case exactly right because he had a magic bell which he always kept next to his right hand. Whenever a law case was being tried, if the guilty party spoke, this bell rang out. David called it his "Bell of Justice."

Now, on this day, his audience chamber was busier than usual, people bustling in and out, bringing their law-suits to the King, asking his advice on many, many matters. Joab the general was there, asking for permission to battle against the Amalekites. Ahitophel was there, questioning the King about his decision to go to Geba to bring the Ark to Jerusalem.

Then the Pleader of the Court brought before the King the case of a man who had been convicted of murder the week before. The Pleader presented new evidence to prove that the two witnesses who had testified against this man had given false evidence.

When the two witnesses stepped up to the throne, the Bell of Justice rang out loud and clear.

"Release the prisoner," King David ordered.

A guard stepped forward and, with one sweep of his sword, struck off the bonds from the man's wrists. The man, dazed but happy, rubbed his bruised wrists, and said,

"Oh thank you, King David. Thank you for sparing my life."

"You may go free," King David said.

Then, pointing to the two witnesses, he said to the guard,

"Now arrest these men. They have sworn falsely under oath. They have committed perjury. Take them to prison."

The two prisoners were led away. And the next case was presented. And the next. And many cases were brought before the King. While he listened intently to each case as it was presented to him, he was thinking impatiently of the songs he would write at night after his sixty breaths of sleep.

Ira sat and watched him, feeling uneasy, still unconvinced that David would be able to awaken after his sixty breaths of sleep. Mephibosheth's story was charming, he thought, but, after all, it was only a legend. No cock would crow exactly sixty breaths after midnight and thus awaken the King.

This problem occupied Ira's mind all through the afternoon session of the court. Then finally court closed. He walked out of the audience chamber with the King and into the King's bedroom.

David walked directly to the east wall where his harp hung. He lifted it off its hook and plucked at the strings. As the melodious sound echoed through the room, David smiled.

"My most precious possession, Ira," he said. "Without my harp I am lost. With my harp, I can sing and write. I would never have composed my poems without the help of this music."

He plucked another chord.

"Listen to my newest song, Ira. This morning as I awakened, I plucked the strings of the harp, and this song rose to my lips:

"I will lift up mine eyes unto the mountains,
From whence shall my help come?
My help cometh from the Lord,
Who made heaven and earth. . . .
Behold, He that keepeth Israel
Doth neither slumber nor sleep."

"Beautiful." Ira nodded. "A gracious song."

King David smiled.

"But David," Ira said. "Your harp puzzles me. Strange that I never noticed this before. Your harp has ten strings. It should have eight, like all other harps."

"There is a special reason for that," David said. "Come, let us sit down. And I shall tell you the story of my wonderful harp."

The two men sat down near the window. David said,

"Generations ago, our father Abraham was commanded by the Lord to sacrifice his young son Isaac."

Ira moved impatiently because he knew that story as well as David did.

"Abraham, grief-stricken though he was, was nevertheless obedient. He took his young son Isaac to Mount Moriah."

"And there he prepared to sacrifice him," Ira interrupted impatiently.

"But," David smiled. "The Lord did not really want Isaac sacrificed. He wanted only to know that Abraham *would* give up his child. And the Lord was satisfied that Abraham was His loyal servant, and He spared Isaac. And in his place, He sent a ram to be sacrificed."

David plucked a chord on the harp.

"When the ram was prepared, father Abraham carefully put aside certain parts of it. These parts he preserved with magic herbs which came from the east. It was the sinews he preserved, and the skin and the horns. The skin and the horns he gave to Isaac to keep the skin to be used by Elijah, for his girdle, and the horn which was used on Mount Sinai at the time of the giving of the Law."

"And the sinews?" Ira asked.

"And the sinews," David continued, "were also given to Isaac who gave them to Jacob when he went to live with Laban. Jacob gave them to Joseph when he found his son alive in Egypt. Joseph gave them to Manasseh who gave them to Serah, daughter of Asher, who gave them to Moses when he led the people of Israel out of Egypt. Just before Moses died, he gave them to Joshua who brought them across the Jordan. And Joshua gave them to Kenaz, the Judge, and then it was handed down from judge to judge until Saul became King of Israel. When Saul appointed me his armor-bearer, and saw how I could drive away his evil spirits with the music of my zither, then Saul gave to me these sinews of the ram which Abraham sacrificed in place of his son Isaac. And I made them into this harp of ten strings."

Ira sighed. "A beautiful story. The ram which God prepared to save our father Isaac, now sings from your harp in devoted praise to Him."

David hung the harp on the wall, and he and Ira then went to the banqueting hall for the evening meal.

After a long and busy evening, the King retired to his bedchamber to sleep. He was eager to fall asleep quickly because he wanted to awaken early to compose new Psalms. Sixty breaths of sleep were all he would allow himself. Then he thought of Mephibosheth's story of the cock crowing at midnight, and smiled. He knew it was only a story, and he would have to rely upon his own will-power to awaken him.

The moon shone brightly through the east window. David undressed and went to bed. In an instant he was fast asleep. And only the moon watched.

The harp hung silently on the wall. No bird's song broke the quiet. No wind rustled amongst the leaves. The king slept.

He breathed ten breaths of sleep. And still the moon watched, and the stars. They blinked and twinkled, and the night air was soft and fragrant with the scent

of roses. The King slept.

He breathed twenty breaths of sleep, and thirty, and forty. And the moon watched, and the stars. Somewhere a child cried out. But it was far off and did not disturb the King's slumber. The King slept.

He breathed fifty breaths of sleep, and fifty-five. And the moon watched, and the stars. The hour approached midnight, and somewhere in the garden a leaf rustled in the faint breeze. The King slept.

He breathed fifty-eight breaths of sleep, and fifty-nine. And the moon watched, and the stars.

And from the heavens came a wind, blowing in through the east window. Lightly the wind touched a string of the harp. It vibrated. It sang out its clear, true note throughout the room.

The King breathed the sixtieth breath of sleep. The lonesome note of the harp reached his ears and vibrated softly as he sat up in bed.

"Ah," David sighed. "The Lord sent the wind to pluck the string of the harp to awaken in me a new song."

He rose, walked to the harp, took it down and began to play. And while he played, he sang:

> *"I made haste and delayed not,*
> *To observe Thy commandment.*
> *At midnight I rise*
> *To give thanks unto Thee."*

Between Sky and Earth

King David and his party were out hunting one day in the woods which divided his kingdom from the land of the Philistines. He was in pursuit of a young deer which loped its way through the underbrush. The King followed it deeper and deeper into the forest.

He was so eager to catch the deer, that he did not notice that he was getting farther and farther away from his party. The sound of the huntsman's horn became fainter and fainter as David went deeper into the woods. Ahead of him the deer dodged for shelter from one tree to another, behind one crag and then another rock, leading David always deeper into the forest.

By now the King was completely cut off from the noblemen who were hunting on the other side of the woods. Not realizing how far he had gone, David kept his eye on the deer until suddenly he reached the far edge of the forest. The deer bounded into a clearing, and just as David was about to cry, "Now I've got you!" the deer loped behind a high boulder, and a voice behind David shouted, "Now I've got you!"

And David felt himself grasped from behind by the collar and lifted clear off his mount. And there he was, dangling in the air.

His horse turned and ran away.

"Finally I've caught you," shouted the voice again.

David twisted his head, trying to see what monster was holding him up in the air; and he saw that it was a giant! In that instant the giant looked like Goliath. But I slew Goliath, David thought desperately. Who can this giant be?

At that moment the giant let go of his collar and dropped him. David fell to the ground with a thud. The wind was knocked out of him and before he had a chance to recover or jump to his feet, the giant's foot, like a huge boulder, came down on David's thigh, pinning him to the ground.

"Now I shall get my revenge!" the giant yelled.

"Wait! Wait!" David shouted, twisting on the ground, trying to get free, and only succeeded in hurting his shoulders as he hit against the rocky earth. "Wait! I am David, King of Israel. Wait!"

"David, King of Israel!" The giant laughed. "Of course, I know who you are. That's why I've captured you, because you are David. And now I shall have my vengeance."

"Who are you? And where am I?" David shouted. "And why do you want revenge on me? I have never seen you before. I have never harmed you. Why do you seek to slay me?"

The giant looked down at him scornfully. "I will take pity on you, little man, and answer you before I dash you to your death. You are in the land of the Philistines."

"The Philistines!" David exclaimed, and now he began to understand too much and too rapidly.

"And I am Ishbi, the brother of Goliath whom you killed. And now I shall avenge my brother."

The giant reached his huge hand down and grasped David by the waist and, holding him out at arm's length, began to stride away. David tried to struggle out of the mighty grasp, but he wriggled as helplessly as a little fly.

"What good will it do if you kill me?" he pleaded. "Let me go and I shall reward you."

Ishbi strode on, not answering.

"I shall give you silver. I shall give you gold," David begged. "Yes, even rubies. Set me free, Ishbi, and I shall give you treasures of rubies and diamonds and pearls."

But on and on Ishbi marched, not answering.

"Perhaps you do not care for jewels or money," David coaxed. "Then I shall give you land. Let me return to my home, Ishbi, and I shall give you fertile wheatfields with water courses and rich barley fields with wells, and a beautiful hillside with a clear-running spring. Just let me go."

But Ishbi did not answer. He strode steadily onward towards the vineyards until he reached a large winepress. Without a word, he flung David down into the winepress.

As David began to fall into the deep press, he prayed and said good-bye to the world, because he knew that the moment he reached the bottom, he would be squeezed to death in the press. But, to his amazement, as his feet touched the bottom of the winepress, the ground beneath the press strangely and wonderfully began to sink down and down, deeper and deeper down, to keep David away from the press so that it would not smash against him. And thus he was kept safe from being crushed in the winepress.

For a moment he leaned against one of the wooden walls of the press, too weak to offer thanks, too exhausted to do more than just be glad he was still alive. He stood there for a few moments, shaking, until he had regained his breath. And then he laughed to himself and said,

"Why am I so grateful for having been saved from being crushed to death? I shall still meet my death here. There is no way for me to climb out. And so here I shall stay and die of thirst and no one in Israel will ever know what became of the King."

For a moment he resigned himself to death. Then his spirits rose again. As long as he was still alive, he thought, if God had performed this miracle of lowering the earth so that he would not be crushed by the winepress, then surely the Lord would find some way of rescuing him.

Meanwhile in the land of Israel, David's cousin Abishai noticed that the day was drawing to a close and that soon it would be the eve of the Sabbath. And so he filled a basin full of water in which to wash his hands and to his amazement the water was not clear. There were drops of blood in the water!

"Blood in the water!" he exclaimed. "That means danger, danger to someone near to me. But who can that be? Who can be in danger?"

He rushed out of his house and into his garden. At that moment a pure white dove came flying towards him. She was weeping and moaning, as doves often do, but this dove's weeping and moaning was loud and piercing and, besides, she was plucking out her own plumes as she flew. She circled around Abishai's head, moaning and wailing, and plucking out her plumes.

"The dove!" Abishai exclaimed. "The dove is a sign to me. She is a symbol of Israel. Does this mean that David, the King of Israel, is in trouble?"

He rushed away, with the dove flying at his side, to the King's palace. And there he found the palace in an uproar. The huntsmen had all returned from the forest, worried and sad. They had lost the King. The King had disappeared into the forest and no one could find him. Everyone stood around gloomily, talking and doing nothing. Abishai rushed away from them, impatient at their helplessness.

He hurried to the King's stables and there he found the King's favorite saddle-beast which had just returned. It was in a lather and panting. It pawed the ground and neighed as though to say, hurry up, someone, ride me! Ride me! Dirt was flying from its hooves as it kept pawing at the ground, tossing its mane wildly. But when Abishai put his hand on the bridle, the saddle-beast became quiet. Abishai swung himself into the saddle.

"I shall go and seek David," he said, "but where? Where shall I go?"

The saddle-beast jerked its head and turned around quickly and began to gallop out of the courtyard.

"Ah, the animal knows where to go," Abishai said, holding the reins more tightly.

And indeed, not only did it know where to go, but for David's sake another miracle happened. When the saddle-beast turned in the direction of the land of the Philistines, the land beneath the feet of the animal drew in and contracted, and with

five wide-spaced gallops and in two seconds, Abishai and the saddle-beast crossed the borders of the land of the Philistines!

The animal stopped. Abishai dismounted and immediately he was confronted by danger. A giantess towered over him, waving a sword and shouting,

"You will never save him. My son Ishbi has thrown him into the winepress."

She pointed to the north and Abishai turned for a quick look. And in that quick look he saw the giant Ishbi standing near the winepress. He turned back, and just in time, for the giantess was about to run him through with her sword.

He plucked his own sword out of its scabbard and began to fence with her.

"Who are you?" he shouted at her, guarding himself from her counter-attack, thrusting his sword this way and that.

"I am Orpah, the mother of the four giants. Your David slew my son Goliath. And now Ishbi and I will be revenged! David shall die! And you too will die!"

At that moment, she lunged forward and he barely had time to back away from the point of her sword. Abishai did not like to do battle with a woman, but he saw that she meant to kill him and then David, and this was no time to quibble about whether the opponent was a man or a woman. So, with one skillful thrust, he pressed his sword into her heart.

And Orpah fell dead.

When Ishbi saw his mother fall to Abishai's sword, he leaned down into the winepress and pulled David up out of it. Then, holding David high, he struck his lance point upward into the ground. And then he threw David high up into the air, so that when he fell, he would fall on the sword and be killed. David went flying up into the sky, trying to twist himself sideways so that when he came tumbling down, he would miss the point of the lance. But he knew it was hopeless. This was certain death. When he fell, he would fall on the lance.

But Abishai came running over and, shouting over the shouts of the giant Ishbi, Abishai pronounced the Divine Name.

And suddenly David was suspended in the air! He hung in the air between the earth and the sky just as if he were standing on firm ground! He could not move upwards. He could not move downwards. He just stood on air halfway between the earth and the sky.

Ishbi, astonished to see David hanging in the air, waited to see him fall. Abishai slew him. The giant Ishbi fell down dead.

Then once more Abishai pronounced the Divine Name.

And David began drifting slowly down from the sky towards the ground and landed gently on his feet.

The two men ran quickly back to the border of the land of the Philistines. The saddle-beast stood there, quietly awaiting them. They mounted together, and the saddle-beast carried them rapidly through the forest until they reached the city of Jerusalem, safe and sound.

The Key Which Unlocked the Rain

When God first created the world, He made seven heavens. In the first were stored all the treasures of snow and ice, of clouds and dew. The whole of this heaven consisted of windows. They were the windows of joy and weeping, of pain and laughing, and hundreds of others. At each window an angel stood guard.

Now one of these was the window of showers and soft rains, and Nuriel was the name of the Angel of Rain. He guarded the Window of Clouds and Showers and helping him were hundreds of other angels. From this window fell all the moistures onto the earth to irrigate the soil and to help the seeds to grow.

Although Nuriel was in charge of the rain as it fell and he could increase it or make it less, he did not have the authority to start it or to stop it, because the key which unlocked the rain window was always in the possession of the Lord.

One day, during the time when David was King of Israel, the angel Nuriel was summoned to the Throne of Glory.

"Nuriel," the Lord said. "Take this key which unlocks the rain. With it lock the Window of Rain securely. Let not one single drop of moisture escape to fall on the earth below."

Nuriel took the Key. And God said,

"When you have done as I have commanded, return the key to Me."

The angel swifted away with the help of his powerful wings, down through all the seven heavens until he reached the first. He hurried past the Windows of Starlight, and of Tears, and of Songs, until he reached the Window of Rain.

It was wide open and a waterfall of rain was descending from heaven to earth.

"Close the window," Nuriel called to his helping angels.

Fifty angels rushed to push the window closed. It was very heavy and required many angels to push and push until it slammed shut. Then Nuriel fitted the huge key into the huge keyhole, turned it, and now the Window of Rain was securely locked.

Nuriel winged his way back to the seventh heaven to the Throne of Glory.

"I have locked the Window of Rain, O Lord," he reported, handing over the key. "Now not a drop will fall onto the ground."

Down on earth, the people did not realize at first what was happening. Nor did King David. He noticed that day that suddenly the rain had stopped and the sun had come out to shine, but that had happened often before. Nor did it seem odd to him the next day, nor the next, that the weather continued sunny, that no rain fell. Truth to tell, he was so busy a King, with such a big kingdom to manage, that he left all matters of weather to his Minister of Weather and all matters of farming to his Minister of Agriculture.

So it was that although day after day and week after week, no rain fell, King David was not aware that anything unusual was happening. But other people began to be disturbed by the drought. The Minister of Agriculture came one day to the Minister of Weather.

"What is wrong in your department?" asked the Minister of Agriculture. "There has been no rain for weeks. The wheat fields are dry. The barley fields are parched. The crops are ruined."

"I cannot understand it myself," said the Minister of Weather. "This should be the rainy season, but all my signs point to 'Clear and Sunny'."

"Well, do something about it!" exclaimed the Minister of Agriculture. "Do something, or we shall have a famine."

"Do something!" retorted the Minister of Weather. "What can I do? I can *study* weather reports and *tell* you whether or not it will rain. But I can't *make* it rain!"

The Minister of Agriculture muttered, "Dreadful. Dreadful. We are faced with hunger. We are faced with famine. Oh, dreadful, dreadful."

"Perhaps," suggested the Minister of Weather, "you might consult the King. Maybe he will call on rain-makers to make the rain to fall."

"Rain-makers!" the Minister of Agriculture exclaimed. "You know that wizards and magicians have been outlawed since King Saul's time."

Nevertheless, he hurried away, and secretly consulted a famous wizard he knew. He promised this man-of-magic a great reward if he could make the rain to fall. He would give him a palace! The wizard, who enjoyed the thought of owning a beautiful palace, set to work immediately. He didn't start with simple magic, but with the most complicated tricks he knew, trying every magic art in his kit, but each trick failed. Each day brought a new disappointment to the wizard and to the Minister of Agriculture, for the rain kept away and the sun continued to shine.

So the Minister of Agriculture sought out a very famous witch, one who was said almost to perform miracles. But she too failed to make rain fall. So the Minister of Agriculture went to another wizard, then another witch, and another, each one failing in turn.

Meanwhile the people had been grumbling for weeks. They saw their fruit in the apple orchards shrivelling up for want of water. They studied the condition of their wells, seeing the water in them sink lower and lower with no rain to replenish them. And they began to fear the approaching famine.

But King David conducted his court day after day, unaware of the danger which threatened the land. There was no lack of anything in the palace. Every day at his dining-table juicy fruits and fragrant roasted meats and fresh-baked bread were brought in and set before him. So he did not know that hunger was stalking the land.

But one day when King David was in his court with his sons, Absalom and Adonijah, Chileab and young Solomon, his secretary came to say that the Minister of Agriculture was asking for an audience.

"Very well," King David said. "Show him in."

The secretary hurried away and came back in a few moments with the Minister of Agriculture who bowed, and said,

"O Your Majesty, forgive me, I pray, for disturbing you. But the matter is of such consequence . . ."

"Very well," King David said. "State the problem."

The Minister of Agriculture said slowly, "Famine. Our land is in the grip of a great famine. Our food supplies are almost completely gone. Our crops are ruined, and the eyes of all Israel are turned to you."

"Indeed!" exclaimed the King. "Why has this happened? Why is our entire food crop spoiled?"

"No rain," the Minister of Agriculture said. "No rain has fallen for months."

"Months!" The King looked at each man in the room. "And I was not informed? Then I must see for myself. Come, Absalom. Come, Adonijah. Come, Chileab. We shall go about the countryside and examine the crops."

He strode out of the room followed by his three older sons, the secretary and the Minister of Agriculture. They all hurried out to the courtyard and after a few quick commands, the chariots were brought and they started out.

Along the road they passed groups of people all standing listlessly, doing nothing. They didn't even bother to hail the King as they stepped out of the way of the chariots. But David looked at them closely. Their clothes looked grey and dusty, and their skins dried up.

"No water," muttered the Minister of Agriculture. "The wells have run dry. The rivers are shrunken to rivulets. The cisterns are empty."

Now they began passing the wheat fields with the wheat stunted and shriveled. They passed brown pastures with no grass. The sun beat down mercilessly on their heads, and the dust of the road parched their throats and stung their eyes. The trees had few leaves and fewer fruits, mostly the bare bark white with dust.

The King, heavy-hearted, ordered the chariots back to the palace. There he assembled his sons in the Throne Room.

"So serious a famine, so widespread a calamity," said the King, "must be a punishment for some sin. Perhaps our people have fallen away from the worship of the One True God. Perhaps in some corners of our land, in some remote villages, the people have become idol-worshippers."

"There is always that danger," Absalom agreed.

"Then let us go and search it out," the King ordered. "Absalom, to the north. Chileab, to the south. Adonijah, to the east. And I shall go to the west and we will all search out any worship of false gods."

The King and the three princes rode off to the four corners of the kingdom. Their search took them everywhere, into every hamlet, into every home. And at the end of four weeks they met again at the palace.

"I have come from the north," said Absalom, "where I find our people worshipping only the True God, the Creator of the world."

"I have come from the south," said Chileab. "And nowhere do I find any idol worship, only reverence for the God of the world, the Father of all men."

"I have come from the east," said Adonijah. "There our people speak only of the Lord of Justice, the true Judge of the world."

"And I myself have come from the west," David, the King of Israel, said. "In no place did I find any worship of a false god, only hymns of thanksgiving to the One True God, the Giver of light and truth."

"Then the cause of the famine," said Absalom, "is not to be found in idol-worship."

"Perhaps, O father," said Adonijah, "perhaps we are being punished because our people are doing evil to each other. Perhaps they lie and steal and murder."

"Then let us go," David said, "and search out the ways of our people."

So again Absalom went to the north and Chileab to the south. Adonijah went to the east and King David to the west. And at the end of four week's time they assembled once more in the palace.

"In the north," Absalom said, "I found only truth. People do not tell lies."

"In the south," Chileab said, "people do not steal. I found everyone dealing honestly with his neighbor."

"In the east," said Adonijah, "the judges are honest and there is no false witness of one man against another."

"And in the west," said King David, "there is no strife or bitterness. There is no killing or murder. People live in friendship and in fair dealing."

"Then," said Adonijah, "sinfulness is not the cause. We must find some cause for this famine."

"Let us then search out amongst our people," King David said, "and see if

perhaps they do not give charity. If they fail in kindness to their fellowmen, if they permit people to starve or go homeless — a lack of charity — ah yes, that could bring this great misfortune."

So again they went their separate ways, and again they returned. In the north, Absalom reported, the people gave charity with a free hand.

"So it is in the south," Chileab said.

"So too in the east," Adonijah reported.

"And in the west, King David said, "the people were so generous that they give away more than they keep. So my sons, the famine comes not from idol-worship, nor from evil living, nor from a lack of charity. It seems that we ourselves will be unable to find the reason for this famine. I shall pray and ask God why. Leave me now, my sons. Leave me to my prayers."

The three young men left the King alone. He locked himself away in his bedchamber. He removed his costly purple-velvet robe. And then he prayed to God. He prayed all night long.

As the night hours passed, and the darkness began to diminish, the King finished his plea in these words:

> "O Lord of the world, Father of all men, Source of Truth and Justice, speak with Thy servant, David. Answer me in this hour of need."

With these words the long prayer was finished, and as the morning star glowed briefly, and a breeze rustled the curtain, David heard a heavenly Voice in answer:

> "David, My son, I hear thy prayer. Hearken to My words. I bid thee remember My servant Saul, King of Israel. Was not Saul anointed with holy oil? Did he not remove the idols from the land? Is he not the companion of Samuel in eternal life? And yet, My son, David, while you dwell in the land of Israel, Saul My servant, the first King of Israel, lies buried outside the land."

The breeze rustled the curtain once more. Then the room was still and quiet. Outside an early bird trilled a note. And inside the King of Israel gave a deep sigh of relief. At last he knew the reason for the famine.

Although dawn had not yet broken, he dressed hurriedly, summoned the sentry and commanded him to awaken his sons and all the nobles, the scholars and priests.

When they were all crowded into the room, the King spoke to them.

"In my prayers I learned the reason for the famine. We have neglected an important duty. We must go and bring back the bodies of Saul and Jonathan from Jabesh-gilead."

Within one hour, the nobles, and the scholars and the priests began their march to Jabesh-gilead. Before them were the King's sons, and at the head of the column, David marched alone.

When they reached Jabesh-gilead, they halted under the tamarisk tree and David ordered his men to open the graves and bring out the coffins of Jonathan and Saul. The two coffins were dug up and placed in chariots. King David himself walked before the chariot carrying the coffin of Saul, and Absalom before the one carrying the coffin of Jonathan.

The procession journeyed back to Jerusalem, going through the whole of the land of Israel until it reached the inheritance of the tribe of Benjamin. And there, amongst the people of his own tribe, Saul, the first King of Israel, was laid to rest, and next to him Jonathan, his son.

At that moment up in the first heaven, the guardian angel of the Window of Rain was commanded to appear at the Throne of Glory. Quickly Nuriel flew away, up through all the heavens, up to the very steps of the Glorious Throne.

"Here now is the key which unlocks the rains, O Nuriel," said the Lord. "Do thou unlock the window."

As quickly Nuriel turned and flew back through all the heavens down to the first, and swifted past all the windows until he reached the Window of Rain.

All the angels of rain waited, ready to spring forward and help. Nuriel, holding the huge key in his hand, rubbed the mist away from the keyhole, thrust in the key, turned it, and unlocked the window. And then fifty angels sprang forward and pulled and pulled at the heavy window, and as they began to pull it open, rain began to seep out of it and then to fall and then to pour down like a torrent to the earth.

Nuriel and the angels pulled the Window of Rain wide, wide, as wide as it would go. And in a few seconds, all the healing, life-giving rain began to descend from the first heaven down to earth.

And David, the King of Israel, and all the people of his kingdom stood out in the open, watching the rain descending, feeling it fall on their faces and wet their hands and soak through their garments, seeing it strike against the earth.

"The rain! The rain has come!"
"The rain! The waters fall once more!"
And King David said in a loud voice,

"The Voice of the Lord is upon the waters;
He giveth rain to the earth."

The Tumbling Priests

One day towards sunset, King David sat in his audience chamber with Nathan the Prophet. The King was leaning back on his Throne, resting.

"I have had a busy day, O Nathan," he said. "I had hundreds of appointments to make. But now I have finished and my court is complete from the highest officer of the guard to the lowest stable boy."

Nathan the Prophet nodded. "Yes, a big task, David. Did you make sure to appoint men from every tribe of Israel?"

"Oh yes," the King answered. "From every tribe. I included noblemen from Reuben's tribe and priests from Levi's tribe and judges from Judah's. Yes, yes, I included everyone whom it was necessary to honor. Every man who should have been placed in a high office was appointed today."

"Then," Nathan said. "I hope that everyone will be satisfied."

"And why shouldn't they be?" demanded King David, sitting up straight.

"Well, for one," Nathan answered, "there is Ahitophel. I know that he is grumbling because you did not appoint him to a high office."

"Ahitophel!" exclaimed David. "Why should he complain? He needs no further appointment. He is already the President of the Sanhedrin. Don't you count being head of the higest court in the land a high office? Isn't that honor enough?"

Nathan the Prophet smiled. *"I would consider it honor enough. But then, I am a Prophet of the Lord and I do not look for these earthly honors. But apparently it matters to Ahitophel. He feels he has been slighted."

"Let him tend to his presiding over the Sanhedrin," David said. "And I shall manage my kingdom without his help."

"You are right, David," Nathan answered. "I mentioned it only to warn you. Watch Ahitophel that he causes you no harm."

"I shall watch him," muttered the King. "I expect him here at any moment."

"Sh! Here he comes," warned Nathan.

A guard opened the door and announced:—

"Ahitophel, the President of the Sanhedrin!"

Ahitophel strode into the room and up to the Throne and he and Nathan and the King greeted each other. David motioned him to a carved oaken chair. Ahitophel seated himself, and David said,

"I have summoned you, Ahitophel, and Nathan, to discuss an important matter. Now that I have established Jerusalem as the capital of my kingdom, I wish to establish it also as the center of the worship of the Lord our God."

"But, Your Majesty," Ahitophel said. "The holy Tabernacle now resides in Geba."

"His Majesty knows that already," Nathan said.

David nodded. "It is to Geba I now wish to go, take the Ark from there, and bring it to Jerusalem. And it is my desire, Ahitophel, that you shall accompany me."

"If the King wishes." Ahitophel made a slight bow.

"But first," King David said, "I wanted to consult you and Nathan. Do you think I do right in bringing the Ark to Jerusalem?"

"Indeed, indeed," agreed Ahitophel. "It is right and seemly that the religious center of the kingdom should be in the capital city."

"You agree then," King David said. "And you, Nathan?"

Nathan spoke slowly. "Yes, I too agree. Here is where the Ark should reside. Jerusalem should be the place of the Sanctuary. For thou, O King, hast long been a deep student of the Holy Law."

"Yes," said David, rather proudly, and a little boastfully. "I study constantly and I can grasp the fine points of the Law."

"David!" Nathan exclaimed. He frowned at the King. "Guard thy speech. Do not boast. You know that all our idle boasting is heard on high."

"The Lord would not punish David," Ahitophel said slyly.

"Oh yes He will," Nathan prophesied. "He will punish him by making him forget a simple law, an easy law, so simple and so easy that even a school child would know it."

"Fear not, dear Nathan," King David said. "I shall forget no laws. But you were right to correct me. I should not have boasted. Now very well then, we all agree that we shall do right to bring the Ark to Jerusalem?"

The other two men nodded.

"Then we shall leave at daybreak tomorrow, Ahitophel. Be prepared to leave with me."

At dawn the next morning, King David and Ahitophel stepped into their chariot. Before them rode David's special vanguard, the four hundred young squires taken captive in foreign wars. Behind the King's chariot rode the King's Guards.

At a signal from the lead of the vanguard, the cavalcade was on the move, on the road to Geba where the Holy Ark was located.

Arrived in Geba, King David sent to summon the priests. In a short while the priests, clad in white garments, accompanied by Levites chanting hymns, came in procession from the Tabernacle and halted before the chariot of the King.

"Greetings, O Priests of the Lord," David said.

"Greetings, O King," they answered.

"O worthy Priests," the King said. "You have served the Lord faithfully and well. You have maintained the Sanctuary with dignity in Geba. Know ye now that I have established Jerusalem as the capital of the kingdom. Now we shall establish Jerusalem as the center of our worship. Let all pilgrims come to Jerusalem to worship in the capital of the kingdom."

"As Your Majesty has decreed," the High Priest said, "so let it be."

All the others nodded.

"Henceforth," King David continued, "the Holy Ark will reside in Jesuralem. Therefore, O Priests, prepare to transport the Ark from Geba to the capital city. We will carry the Ark in a wagon."

Ahitophel, standing behind the King, said nothing, but he smiled. No one saw him smile.

"Order the wagons!" King David commanded.

The Chief of Transports rushed away to commandeer the wagons. The four hundred young squires led the way to the Tabernacle. Behind them came the King and Ahitophel, and behind them the priests. The procession moved forward to the Tabernacle, entered, and continued on up to the altar.

King David motioned to the High Priest to step forward.

"You and your assistant," he said, "will now remove the Ark from the Holy of Holies. You will carry it out of the Tabernacle and place it in the wagon."

"As Your Majesty wishes," the High Priest said.

He motioned to his assistant and they stepped forward together to the Holy of Holies. The High Priest pushed aside the cover. He put out his hand to grasp the Ark and his assistant put out his hands to receive it from the High Priest.

Just as the High Priest touched his hand to the Ark, suddenly, he and his assistant were jerked around, their bodies twisting and shaking, their feet left the ground, and then, as if a giant hand were pulling them on strings, they were thrown high up into the air. Twisting and turning, they began to fall, and then came tumbling down!

Two other priests rushed to help them up from the ground. They struggled to their feet, unhurt but dazed and embarrassed. Everyone stood mystified, except King David.

Angrily he spoke. "Ye must be sinful priests. You are proven unworthy to touch the Ark. Step aside."

The High Priest and his assistant were silent and ashamed. They bowed their heads, and slipped back through the ranks to the rear.

Then said David, "If there be two priests among you who know that they have

not sinned, let them step forward."

One tall priest approached the Holy of Holies without hesitation. Then, slowly, another priest, short and stout and red-faced, came forward.

"Remove the Ark," King David ordered.

The tall priest put his hand on the Ark, and in an instant, he and the short, stout priest were sent whirling around, twisting and turning, as if a violent wind blew them off the ground and up into the air, and then like a tornado, twisting and turning, tumbled them down to to the ground.

They too were unhurt, but shaken up and embarrassed. They shuffled to their feet and without a word hurried away to hide in the crowd of their fellow priests.

King David turned and glared from priest to priest and each one dropped his eyes before the King's accusing look.

"Are then all my priests unworthy?" David shouted. "Isn't there one priest pure enough to touch the Ark? Is there no one who knows why these priests are being tumbled about?"

No one answered the King. He turned to Ahitophel who was looking at the Ark, a slight smile twisting his lips. But he said nothing.

And then David remembered Nathan the Prophet warning him to beware of Ahitophel.

"Ahitophel," David said. "Have you nothing to say?"

Ahitophel smiled and shrugged his shoulders. "Let the King ask this question of those he has set in high offices. The King chose to overlook me. Then why now does the King turn to me for help?"

David turned away from Ahitophel and said,

"He who knows how to stop this disgraceful performance and does not speak up, that person will be surely punished."

A tall, thin priest began to move forward, but Ahitophel stopped him and said to the King.

"If it please, Your Majesty. The fault lies not with the priests. The fault lies with the King himself."

"With me?" King David asked.

"With you, Your Majesty," Ahitophel said. "Have you, perhaps, forgotten the simple law which states that whenever the Ark of the Lord is to be moved, it must be carried on the *shoulders of the priests?* Do you not recall that in the desert, Moses permitted the sons of Gershon two wagons and the sons of Meran four wagons, to transport the heavy portions of the Tabernacle, the boards and the bars and the poles. But when the Ark was moved, Moses ordered the Levites, the sons of Kehath, to carry it on their *shoulders*. Do you not remember? Yet you have instructed that the Ark itself now be carried to Jerusaslem in a wagon. The Tabernacle may be so transported, but not the Ark."

"You are right, Ahitophel!" King David exclaimed. "How could I have forgotten this simple law?"

"Your forgetting was a punishment," Ahitophel said, "for the sin of boasting. Didn't Your Majesty boast, in the hearing of Nathan the Prophet and myself, that you knew every portion of the Holy Law?"

"Yes!" David acknowledged. "I did boast. And Nathan the Prophet did warn me that for such a boast I would forget a simple law. And I did!"

He turned back to the priests.

"O Priests, the fault is not in you but in me. I beg the pardon of the Priests of the Tabernacle for having forgotten so simple a law and for having caused this embarrassment. Now we shall take the Ark to Jerusalem, but we shall have it carried on the shoulders of the priests."

He signalled to the Chief of Transports. "Dismiss the wagons!" he ordered.

The wagons were rushed away, out of sight. Then King David motioned to the High Priest and his assistant, to the tall and the short, stout priest with the red face, to come forward. They steppped up and King David said,

"You will carry the Ark on your shoulders."

The High Priest placed his hand on the Ark. He waited. Everyone held his breath. But nothing happened. He and the three other priests remained standing firmly on the ground. There was no more tumbling about!

The High Priest lifted out the Ark and placed it on the shoulders of all four. And everyone present breathed a sigh of relief.

The vanguard of the four hundred squires started off, and behind them came King David and Ahitophel, and behind them came the priests carrying the Ark from Geba to Jerusalem. Their fellow priests marched behind the Ark, singing their chants all the way.

As they approached their journey's end, and saw Jerusalem before them, they chanted the words:

> *"Lift up your heads, O Ye gates,*
> *That the King of Glory may come in!"*

Thus did Jerusalem become the city of pilgrimage, and the home of the Sacred Ark.

The Talking Shard

At the Creation of the world, after the earth and heavens had been formed, and the dry land and the sea had been separated, there remained vast quantities of water left over for which there was no use. They were wild, tumbling waters, foaming and boiling waters that frequently flooded the earth. And so, in those ancient days, there were many parts of the world where men could not live because the wild waters would sweep away everything, the houses that were built and the fields which were planted.

Then came that great day on Mount Sinai when God spoke the words:—

"I am the Lord thy God."

Then the mountain trembled and the earth shook and the mighty abyss opened up deep in the body of the earth. And the Lord said,

"Into this abyss will I draw the wild waters of Creation."

So, deep into this abyss He pushed all these wild and uncontrolled waters. But that cavity wasn't deep enough and immediately the waters began pushing and rising to the top, threatening to rush out in mighty torrents.

To the angel Ya'asriel standing nearby, the Lord said,

"I shall have to keep the wild waters from flooding the earth. I shall have to put a cover over the abyss."

Whereupon He picked up a broken fragment of clay, a flat piece dried hard in the sun, a shard, and this He placed on top of the abyss.

But the waters in the abyss were too strong for this fragile piece of clay and they came rushing out and washed the shard away. Then the Lord beckoned to Ya'asriel and said,

"Bring your seventy pencils. Inscribe My Name on this shard."

From under his left wing where he kept them, Ya'asriel pulled out his seventy pencils, one for each of the seventy languages of the world. He picked up the shard and on it, in indelible letters wrote the Divine Name. Then he handed the shard to God Who pushed all the waters back into the abyss and over it He placed the shard. This time the shard remained securely in place.

"Now that My Name is on the shard," said the Lord, "it will remain firm. Now all the waters of the abyss are safely held in check. Never will they overflow the earth unless . . ."

"Unless?" Ya'asriel asked.

"Unless," said the Lord, "a certain child of Adam standing by the shard of clay will utter an oath of evil and untruth."

Hundreds of years passed, and in all that time no one ever saw the shard which covered the abyss because, as the seasons changed and the earth shifted from spot to spot, more and more soil covered the shard until it became lost to sight. There it was, safe, deep under the earth, holding back, by the power of God's Name, all the raging waters from the days of Creation.

Centuries passed until the day came when David was King of Israel.

One day the King said to Ahitophel, the President of the Sanhedrin,

"Ahitophel, I have decided to build a Temple to the Lord here in Jerusalem, and on the best hill of the city. Come with me, good friend, and let us search to find a spot worthy of the Holy Temple. Come, my friend."

But Ahitophel was not truly a friend. He only pretended friendship. Actually he was plotting some way to overthrow David so he himself could be King. While David was speaking, Ahitophel came quickly to the decision that this very search for a place for the Temple could be used to harm David in some way. So he went with King David on this search and soon an opportunity arose for him to make trouble.

The King favored a certain hill. It was a good choice, but Ahitophel objected. He chose a different hill, and David was willing to accept Ahitophel's choice.

Now it happened that deep beneath this very spot chosen by Ahitophel lay the ancient shard bearing the Divine Name protecting the waters of the abyss.

King David gave orders to the Royal Engineers to begin excavations at once. He was so impatient to begin, that even before the architects could start their drawings, he ordered the engineers to start digging the foundations. For many years David had dreamed of building the Temple and now his dream was coming true. He did not return to the palace. He stood at the side of the royal engineers, watching the workmen digging in the ground.

All day long the diggers came hurrying, carrying shovels and pickaxes. Packmules were led to the spot bringing sacks of cement. The surveyors started measuring the ground, and the architects began drawing plans. Everyone went busily to work.

Soon the light began to fade and the darkness approach. The work had to stop until the next morning, and David reluctantly returned to the palace.

Early the next morning, even before the sun was shining, King David hurried to the site of the new building. There he found the royal engineers already hard at the job, with the workmen digging away.

They dug and they dug, hour after hour, until finally they had gone down a very great distance. Sudenly one of the royal engineers exclaimed,

"Look what I have found!"

"One moment!" King David cried in turn. "Look what *I* have found!"

He reached down and, right at the edge of the abyss, picked up a pot. He raised it for all to see.

"Be careful," one of the older engineers warned. "We have dug very deep. We have come to the edge of the abyss. Be careful what you pick up, Your Majesty."

"Oh, there's no harm in this," King David said, examining the pot closely. "I do believe I have found a marvelous treasure. This must be the pot of magic herbs."

"Magic herbs?" Ahitophel said, having just joined the group. "Whose magic herbs?"

"Balak's, the King of Moab," David explained. "That famous magician of olden times. This must be the pot of magic herbs which he placed at the abyss. What a wonderful find!"

He turned to a workman and handed him the pot of magic herbs.

"Take this to my palace. Give it to the royal physician. Tell him to keep it for me."

As the workman, clutching the precious pot of magic herbs, hurried away, King David turned to the royal engineer.

"Now," he asked. "What did you find?"

"That," the engineer said, pointing to the shard.

"That?" David said. "Why, that is only a shard, just a piece of broken clay." He bent over to pick it up.

And a voice rose from the clay, saying, "Do not touch me!"

"It speaks!" the royal engineer exclaimed. "The clay speaks!"

"That cannot be," King David said. "It is some kind of a trick one of you is playing. A clump of clay cannot talk."

"Indeed I *can* talk," the shard said. "And I say to you, David, King of Israel, do not pick me up."

"If you can speak, O Shard," the King said, "then you can also answer my questions. Tell me, why should I not pick you up?"

And the Shard answered, "Because I rest upon the abyss."

"Since when?"

"Since the day when, on Mount Sinai," said the Shard, "the Voice of the Creator spoke and said, 'I am the Lord thy God.' The earth was frightened and she shook and quivered and created the huge cavern that is the abyss. And all the raging waters of Creation rushed into the great cavern. Then I, the Shard of Clay, carrying the Name of God, was put here to cover up that abyss."

Ahitophel laughed. "Now indeed this is a likely tale. How could one little broken piece of clay hold back strong, rushing waters? Pick it up, King David. Pick up the shard."

Now Ahitophel was purposely causing trouble. He wanted the King to do something that he, a learned scholar who knew about such things, hoped would bring misfortune to the King. Then he, Ahitophel, could snatch David's crown off his head and set it on his own.

David hesitated. And Ahitophel urged him.

"I know about these things, Your Majesty. Trust me. I swear to you that the Shard speaks lies."

As soon as he uttered this false statement, the letters of the Lord's Name trembled and twitched themselves loose, rose from the Shard, and flew away. The Shard rolled away. And the abyss was uncovered!

Soon was heard the rush of mighty waters and in a moment the crest of a dark wave rose up and began to sweep into the excavation which had been dug. Then another dark wave rose, then another, until all the waters in it began roaring, pushing, tumbling, racing to get out and flood the earth.

Everyone rushed towards higher land, dry land, except Ahitophel and the royal engineer, and except King David himself. He picked up the shard. The waters were tumbling out and soon they covered David's feet and then his ankles.

Above the roaring of the flood, King David shouted, "Who knows how to stop the flow of these waters?"

Ahitophel knew, but he stood quietly by, saying nothing.

And the waters rose as high as their knees.

"O little Shard," King David said. "Do you know how to stop these destroying waters?"

"That I do not know, O David," the Shard answered. "But call thou upon the angel Ya'asriel whose hand it was that placed me here. Perhaps he can help you."

The waters rose as high as their hips.

David lifted his head towards the heavens, and called, "Ya'asriel! Ya'asriel, Angel of the Lord. Do thou come to my help. I plead with thee, Ya'asriel, come quickly. Help!"

The waters rose as high as King David's chest. Suddenly he saw at his side the angel Ya'asriel.

"I heard thee call, O David," Ya'asriel said. "And I have come to help thee."

"I thank thee, Ya'asriel," David said. "But hurry please, hurry. There is not a moment to lose. The waters are reaching up to my throat."

Ya'asriel pulled out from under his left wing his seventy pencils. Then from King David's hand he took the Shard. And on the Shard he wrote once more the sacred letters of the Name of God. Then he cried out,

"O ye raging waters, wild waters of Creation. Return to the abyss where the Lord had placed you."

Instantly the waters began to drop. There was a great rumbling, a great tumbling, a great roaring as the waters rushed to get back into the abyss. They dropped away from David's neck, then his chest, and then splashed against the big rocks. Then they dropped away from David's hips, then from his knees, and they poured fast and faster back into the huge crater which was the abyss. And still they rushed, to get back to safety now that God's Name was there to get them under control and keep them in check. And they left David's ankles and then ran off the ground and into the deep cavity.

"Now the waters are gone, O David," Ya'asriel said.

But before David could thank him, the Shard cried out, "But now they are sinking too low! O Ya'asriel, look! See! The waters are sinking, sinking. They are going too low. The wells will be empty and the fountains dry up."

"Let me try to make them rise again," King David said.

The Shard and Ya'asriel said together, "Hurry, David, hurry."

"Let me sing a song," David said. "Let me try to bring the waters up to fill the wells and the fountains, yet stay in the abyss."

"Sing, David," cried the Shard. "The waters are receding too far!"

"Sing, David," cried Ya'asriel. "Or the waters will disappear from sight."

King David raised his voice and sang above the roar of the waters.

"The floods have lifted up their voice,
The floods lift up their roaring.
Above the voices of many waters,
The mighty breakers of the sea,
The Lord on high is mighty."

"Now the waters are restored!" Ya'asriel cried.

"Now, King David," the Shard said. "Place me back on the mouth of the abyss."

And King David placed the Shard on top of the abyss. And the waters were contained therein for all time.

House of David

Nathan the Prophet awoke one morning from a dream in which God had told him to journey to Jerusalem to take a message to David, the King of Israel. Nathan looked out of the window of his house in Bethlehem that morning and shook his head in impatience when he saw that it was still raining. The rainy season of the year had not come to an end, and it was impossible to travel now because the roads would be too muddy. There was nothing to do but wait until the rains stopped and the road dried out. By then it would be almost time for the festival of Passover. If Nathan waited until then, he would have a great deal of company on his travels. On the roads would be pilgrims taking their paschal lambs to Jerusalem.

At the end of three weeks, when the rainy season finally ended, all the pilgrims from Bethlehem began their preparations to go to the Sanctuary. And Nathan started out with them, travelling the road to the capital.

After many days he reached Jerusalem and went directly to the palace where he was taken at once to the King.

"Nathan," David exclaimed. "How glad I am to see you."

"And I to see you, David," answered Nathan.

"I did not expect you so soon," the King said. "Do you have urgent business in Jerusalem?"

"Yes," Nathan answered. "I come on a matter of great importance, something I must discuss with you."

"I am always happy to discuss any matter with you," David said. "But now you are weary from your travels and must rest. We shall talk later, after the evening meal."

The daylight hours passed. Dusk came, and with it the evening meal. In the banqueting hall were King David and the Prophet Nathan, and David's sons, Absalom and Adonijah, Chileab and Solomon. Nathan brought them all the news of Bethlehem. And they gave him all the news of Jerusalem.

When the meal ended, the King and Nathan left the men of the court and strolled together through the pavilions out to the water gardens in the grove of myrtle trees. And David said,

"You know well, Nathan, that all the affairs of the kingdom run smoothly."

Nathan nodded. "Now that the famine has ended."

"Yes," David said. "Now that the famine has ended." He sighed. Then he continued, "It is a long, long time since that day when Samuel the Prophet anointed me King. Many years have passed, busy years. I fought many wars. I composed many psalms."

Nathan nodded again. "Yes, David," he agreed. "A busy life, a busy life indeed."

Then King David laughed. "But don't think that just because I am growing old, I am through with my work. Oh no. Jerusalem is well established as the center of the kingdom. I have had the Ark transported from Geba to Jerusalem. And now, there is one thing more I want to do. I wish to build a Temple to the Lord in which the Holy Ark shall be permanently placed."

"Ah yes," Nathan said. "A Temple to the Lord."

"You don't sound enthusiastic," David complained. "Don't you approve, Nathan?"

"Of course I approve," Nathan said. "But you cannot rush into such a great undertaking. There are many problems which must be solved first."

"Nathan," the King said irritably. "You are fencing with me. I am prepared to cope with any problem which may arise."

"Have you thought of the vast amount of money you will need?" Nathan asked.

"Of course I have," David said.

"You have?" asked Nathan. "Yet let me remind you that you have had to engage in many wars, expensive wars, in which you used up vast sums of money. I know that the famine which has just ended has been costly. Your treasury must be empty."

"Empty!" King David exclaimed. "You think it is empty? I shall show you. Early in the morning I shall take you to my treasury, and I shall show you the treasures I have piled up there, and then you shall see whether or not I have money enough to build the Temple."

"Very well," Nathan agreed. "We shall go to your treasury in the morning. And now, Your Majesty, if you will permit me to retire? I am very tired from my journeys."

"Very well," David said rather brusquely. "Go to your rest if you are tired."

David frowned in disappointment. He had expected that Nathan would be enthusiastic about his plans and would want to stay up and talk for hours about the building of the Temple. And because he was disappointed he permitted Nathan to retire, still without having asked him why he had come to Jerusalem.

The two men parted for the night, and met again early the next morning at breakfast. King David was polite to his guest but hurried him through the meal. He ordered his chariot and in it rushed Nathan off to the treasury.

As they dismounted, the guards in front of the treasury saluted. The King drew out a large key from his pouch and with it opened the heavy bronze door. He led Nathan down a long corridor, then past a room of windows, then down a flight of stairs to the underground passage where there was a vault with a heavy iron door.

David stopped in front of this door and said to Nathan,

"When I was yet a lad, I encountered the giant Goliath in battle. And with God's help, as you remember, I slew this hero of the Philistines. Upon my return from the battle, the women of Saul's court came running to meet me, and at my feet they threw their jewels. They gave me their gold and their silver, and all these years I have been hiding this wealth. I have waited to use these treasures for the building of the Temple."

David opened the heavy iron door and went inside, followed by Nathan. The Prophet looked about and saw a vast quantity of jewels, diamonds and pearls and rubies, rings of every description. He saw huge piles of gold coins in one corner, bracelets and earrings and precious stones of all kinds.

"Yes," he said then to David. "You have enough wealth here with which to build the Temple."

David smiled. "Then you can see for yourself that with all this wealth at my disposal, there is no hindrance to my plans."

"But David," asked Nathan. "Why did you not use this wealth to end the famine sooner?"

"Oh Nathan," David said impatiently. "Why do you keep talking of the famine? It is true I could have used this money to end the famine, but I was saving it for this very reason, and anyway, I ended the famine as soon as I could."

"Still," Nathan said stubbornly. "This money should have been used to help your people."

"I must disagree with you, Nathan," the King said stiffly. "I felt that this treasure was a sacred trust to be used only for the house of God. Hear me now, Nathan. Once, many, many years ago, when I was guarding my sheep, I was caught on the horns of a wild buffalo, a Re'em. I faced certain death. And I vowed then that if the Lord would save me, I would some day build a Temple to do Him honor. My prayers were heard and answered, and I was rescued. Now I shall pay that vow which I made so long ago."

"Very well," Nathan said quietly. "There is no use my insisting that this money should have been used when our country was in trouble, since the famine is now over. Therefore I agree, you have overcome the first obstacle since you have this vast wealth. Now there is another obstacle."

"Truly, Nathan, you are being unfriendly," King David said. "You are not trying to help me. All you do is to find reasons to keep me from fulfilling my sacred vow."

"Come, David," said Nathan. "Do not act like a child. You yourself told me the trouble you had when you and Ahitophel went to look for a site for the Temple, how you uncovered the shard from the abyss and the waters of Creation rose and threatened to flood the whole earth. Perhaps that was a sign from the Lord that you are not to build the Temple."

"No, no, Nathan," David said earnestly. "Do not look upon that mishap as a sign from heaven. That site at which I found the shard was not of my choosing. That was the place which Ahitophel had chosen."

"Nevertheless," persisted Nathan. "You could not find a proper location."

"Ah, but I have!" David exclaimed. "Come with me, Nathan, and I shall show you the very place where the Temple is to be built."

He led the Prophet out of the vault, up the stairway, through the corridor of windows, out through the bronze door, which he locked. They got into the chariots and drove away.

There was no conversation during this ride. Nathan was casting about in his mind for the proper words to use to David, to bring him the message he had received in his dream in Bethlehem. And David was now even more offended that the Prophet stubbornly opposed his plan. Surely the Prophet should want him to build the Temple and not oppose it so much.

And so they rode in silence, through Jerusalem, until they came to Mount Moriah.

They descended from the chariot and the King led Nathan up a stony path, winding their way amongst the rocks and through low bushes, until they reached the very top. And here they felt close to the sky. And from here they could see the whole city of Jerusalem.

Nathan shook his head and sighed, and David said anxiously,

"Do you not approve, O Nathan? Do you not like this crest at the top of Mount Moriah?"

"Oh yes, David," Nathan said quietly. "I approve. I approve highly of Mount Moriah."

"Well then?" David said impatiently, grasping Nathan's arm. "Well then? What is your objection now?"

"David, my friend," Nathan said. "I have been with you many hours now, and you have not yet asked me why I have come to Jerusalem."

"I beg your pardon, Nathan," David said stiffly, "for permitting my enthusiasm to run ahead of my good manners. You are right. I should have kept back my plans of building the Temple, until Nathan had stated his business. We shall return to the palace at once."

Nathan interrupted him. "I can tell you here, on the top of Mount Moriah, David. My business with you, O King, concerns precisely your plans to build the Temple. So there is no better place to tell you than here on this mountain top."

"Well then," David said. "Why are you not more enthusiastic?"

"I am enthusiastic about the Temple, David," insisted Nathan. "But I cannot be enthusiastic about *your* building it."

"Indeed," David began to say angrily, but Nathan interrupted him.

"Just before I came to Jerusalem," he said, "I received a revelation. In my dreams the Lord came to me and said, 'Nathan, My servant, go to Jerusalem and tell My son David that he is not to build the Temple."

"Not to build the Temple!" David cried, grasping Nathan's arm. "Nathan, you don't know what you're saying. Does God forbid us to build Him a Temple?"

Nathan shook his head. "No, David. God desires us to build a Temple. But not you are to build it. Solomon, your son, is to build the Temple to the Lord."

"I am forbidden to build the Temple?" David said. "I cannot believe it. Tell me why, O Prophet? Has the Lord found me unworthy?"

"You are not to build the Temple," Nathan said, "because if you build it, God then would decree for your sake that the Temple should be eternal and indestructible."

David looked dazedly at Nathan. "But what is wrong with that? Wouldn't it be good if God's Temple lasted forever and could not be destroyed?"

"Perhaps, David," Nathan said. "But the Lord Who knows all things, knows that, in time to come, the people will sin. Perhaps they will do many things which will be wrong. They will have to be punished and there are one of two punishments which the Lord would choose, either to destroy the people and let the Temple stand, or to destroy the Temple and let the people live."

David did not answer. He was sunk in gloom. He had set his heart on this building. And Nathan's message was a great blow to his plans. He was crushed. He had almost no voice left to utter any more complaints.

Nathan continued, "The Lord told me to hasten and tell you not to build the Temple, David, and it is well that I have hastened, because you are always impatient. The moment you have an idea, you rush to execute it. If you had already hired laborers and begun to dig the ground, your disappointment would have been still greater than it is now."

"My disappointment is great enough," David said gloomily. "I am the despised of the Lord. He has no love for me."

"David, David," Nathan chided. "You are no child to sit and sulk when a wish of yours is not granted, even if it be a wish as splendid as building the Temple."

"No, I am not a child," David retorted, "and I am not sulking. But I am bitterly disappointed. I had hoped that when our people pray to the God of Abraham, Isaac and Jacob, they will be praying in the Temple of David. But it seems that I am not worthy of that great honor."

"Hear me, David," said Nathan. "Because you wished to build the Temple and for your many other merits, the Lord will now give you two great blessings."

"Two blessings?" David said. "I would be satisfied with one."

"Nevertheless, you shall have two," Nathan said. "The Lord will include your name with the names of the fathers, and when the people pray to 'The God of Abraham, Isaac and Jacob,' in their benedictions they will say, to 'God, the Shield of David'."

" 'God, the shield of David!' " David repeated. " 'God, the shield of David!' This is a great blessing, Nathan. This is blessing enough."

"Then you will no longer grieve over your disappointment of not building the Temple?" Nathan asked, smiling.

"No." David smiled. "No, I shall not grieve over it. I am happy to know that my son Solomon will be permitted to build it. And I shall be blessed indeed whenever people will pray to 'God, the shield of David.' "

Then Nathan said, "You will have yet one more blessing, David. Although the Temple will be built by your son Solomon, it will always be known as — 'The House of David.'"

David stretched out his hands towards Nathan, and said, "The House of David! The Shield of David in the House of David. I am consoled, O Nathan. I am doubly blessed."

The Frog's Rebuke

There was a quiet pond in King David's apple orchard. And in that pond lived an old frog.

One day, as usual, he climbed out of the water, seated himself cross-legged on a moss-covered rock at the edge of the pond to sun himself. It was quiet there and he was enjoying his solitude. Then, to his annoyance, he heard the sound of voices.

As they came closer, he recognized them. They belonged to King David's teachers, Ira and Mephibosheth. Now this frog had lived in this pond ever since David the King had built his palace in Jerusalem years ago, and so he knew every person connected with the King's court. Some people he did not like and when they strolled near his pond, he would plop off his rock into the water with a loud "Kerplunk!" Then he would splash loudly in the water and croak at the top of his voice until he drove those people away to look for a quieter place. Some people he liked, as he did Ira and Mephibosheth, and whenever they were near, he remained perfectly still, because he enjoyed listening to their conversation.

Now, of course, the person he liked to listen to best of all was the wise and the noble King. But if David were not there, then next best, he liked to hear Ira and Mephibosheth talk.

So now he gave one little croak of satisfaction and then sat very quiet, listening to these two wise men. Mephibosheth was speaking.

"How nice and quiet it is here."

"It won't be quiet long," Ira said. "King David has ordered all the priests to appear here in the apple orchard after the mid-day meal. And look, the priests are beginning to come."

Mephibosheth and Ira turned to watch the priests approach, greeting each one by name. With them came Jehoshaphat, the King's recorder, and Sheva, the King's scribe.

The frog saw them coming and gave a little croak of excitement, but no one heard him. Then he sat motionless, his eyes popping to see everything, his ears straining to hear everything.

"Here comes David," Ira said suddenly.

"Here comes the King," said Mephibosheth.

At the approach of the King, the air was filled with respectful greetings from the priests.

David the King came walking towards them with a quick, springy step. A smile lighted his face. Behind him came an attendant carrying two large silken pillows. And behind the attendant marched five pages. Each page was dressed in a white satin suit. Each one was carrying a strange object on a white satin pillow.

The frog blinked and sat up straighter.

"Greetings." David smiled at all the men assembled before him. "I thank you, gentlemen, for hearkening to my summons to appear here today. For I have a matter of great interest to bring before you."

He gave a signal and every person seated himself on the grass. The King's attendant placed the two silken pillows on the ground right next to the rock on which the frog was perched. So the frog, on his moss-covered rock, had an excellent, front-row seat throughout the afternoon next to David himself.

The six pages carrying the white satin pillows stood at attention behind the King, and Jehoshaphat the recorder, recorded the proceedings. Then the King spoke.

"All through my life, as a shepherd, as a general, as a King, I have always composed songs in praise of the Lord. And every song which came into my mind, I have written down, as you well know."

The frog croaked once.

"But what you do not know," David said, "is that for a long time now I have been inventing musical instruments."

"New musical instruments! Indeed!" Ira sat up straight, astonished. He thought he knew everything about the King.

"In truth?" asked Mephibosheth, a little miffed because he thought he knew everything about the King.

But the frog chuckled to himself. He could have told them! Many an early dawn, many a late twilight, many a star-lit night he had sat on his rock near the pond listening to the King try out one new instrument after another.

"All string-instruments," King David said. "And here they are."

He motioned to the pages to come forward. As each one bowed before him, the King picked up an instrument from the pillow and plucked at a string. Of the first he said,

"This is the Mehiloth."

And then he named them in turn: — the Sheminith, the Gittith, the Muth-labben and the Ayeleth-ha-Shahar. The Priests and Levites gathered around him, examining each instrument, exclaiming over them. And one Levite, a slender one with long, sensitive fingers, said,

"How I should like to be able to play this Gittith."

"That you shall," King David said. "That is my plan, to teach the Levite-Priests to play these instruments."

"Oh, it will be an honor and a joy too," said the slender priest with the sensitive fingers.

"That spells trouble for me," a heavy-set priest said, shaking his head. "I should be all thumbs."

So should I, thought the frog to himself.

David smiled at the heavy-set priest. "You need not be troubled. Not all of you

will learn to play the instruments, only a few. And those few will teach them to their pupils. And the rest of you . . ."

He paused to glance at each one, to smile as if he were unwilling to share his secret too soon. Then he continued,

"And the rest of you wll learn to *sing* my songs."

"Good, splendid!" cried out a priest with a deep, pleasant baritone.

"I shall like that," said a tenor-voiced priest.

"But what shall I do?" begged a red-faced priest. "I cannot sing. I cannot carry a tune. I sing all on one note."

Just like me, thought the frog. I just croak along on one note.

But the King smiled at the red-faced priest.

"Don't worry," he said. "You will have your share of the enjoyment. You may *write* the copies of the music."

The red-faced prest beamed because he was famous for his beautiful penmanship.

"All these hymns," Ira said, "will beautify our services on the Sabbath and the festivals."

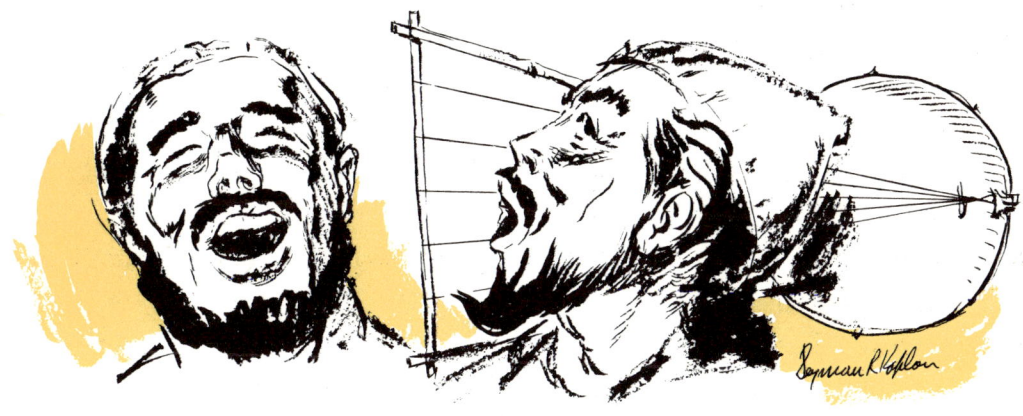

"We must start immediately," said the High Priest.

King David nodded. "On the morrow. After the morning prayers, we shall begin our lessons in music. And now, honored priests, I have one more thing to tell you."

David's voice had become solemn. The men bent their heads to listen. The frog sat up straighter.

"I am thankful to the Lord," David said, "that in recent years I have been freed from wars and dangers, and I have had time to work without interruption on my psalms."

135

Mephibosheth bowed, and said, "If I may be permitted a boldness. You have never really ceased writing your psalms since first you sang, 'The Lord is my Shepherd'."

David smiled. Then he said, "This dawn, before the crowing of the cock, I have finished composing my final psalm."

"This is cause for rejoicing!" cried Jehoshaphat.

"Indeed, it is!" Sheva exclaimed.

"Read it to us, David," suggested Ira. "Sing us your last psalm."

David picked up the Gittith and plucked a chord. A bird nearby answered with a trill. And David sang,

"Hallelujah.
　Praise God in His sanctuary; ...
　Praise Him for His mighty acts;
　Praise Him with the blast of the horn; ...
　Praise Him with the clanging cymbals;
　Let every thing that hath breath praise the Lord.
　Hallelujah."

As David finished, everyone exclaimed in admiration.

"Beautiful."

"A fitting finale for your Book of Psalms."

"We must celebrate," declared Sheva. "I shall hasten to the royal cooks and order a banquet for this evening."

"And I shall hasten to the royal bakers," Mephibosheth said. "We shall celebrate! We shall honor the King!"

David laughed. "Just a moment, my good friends. These songs were written in praise of the Lord, not in honor of David. You must not praise me merely for writing down what the Lord has put into my heart."

"No modesty now," Mephibosheth said. "This is no time for our good King to be so humble. Tonight the Court will ring with song and praise of our King, of David, the Sweet Singer of Israel. Come, let us go and prepare the banquet."

As the priests began to hurry away, and Mephibosheth turned to go with them, Ira stopped him and said,

"Please, Mephibosheth, please take care of the arrangements for the banquet. I have an important matter I must discuss with the King."

"Certainly," Mephibosheth said. "I'll hurry to the cooks and the bakers, and I shall arrange the entire banquet. Leave it to me."

He hurried away. And Ira said,

"Jehoshaphat, Sheva. You remain."

Then he turned to King David.

"O King, while the others rush away to prepare a banquet which will be forgotten tomorrow or next week, I want to suggest something, Your Majesty, whose effects will last longer, much longer than such a feasting and celebrating. Your songs must live forever. I desire to arrange for the copying of the psalms. I wish to arrange to have them bound together as a book to preserve them for the future."

"Oh no," David said. "There is no need to preserve my poetry that it shall live beyond my lifetime. There will be other poets whose songs people will sing in generations to come."

"There will never be a better poet," said Ira.

Sheva and Jehoshaphat nodded their agreement.

"Do not be so modest, dear King," Ira said. "Let Jehoshaphat and Sheva arrange to copy your songs on parchment. Then they will bind them in fine, soft leather."

"Very well," David interrupted. "Arrange it if you like, Ira. And now please, I should like to be alone for contemplation."

The three men withdrew, and the King, with a sigh, rested his back against a tree.

The frog sighed too, glad that he had witnessed this day's proceedings. And he thought to himself, how modest King David is. But how nice that his friends wish to do him honor.

King David was thinking the same thing, how kind his friends were to celebrate the completion of his Psalm Book with a banquet. He was happy about that, but he was happier that Ira was arranging to have the poetry copied and bound and saved for future generations. The more he thought about it, the more excited he became. In his excitement he jumped to his feet and began to pace beside the stream. Suddenly he began to pray aloud,

"O Lord, I have written my hymns of praise to Thee. Not for my glory but for Yours, O Heavenly Father, do I wish them to be remembered. Grant, O King of Kings that my psalms may be read whenever Israel may worship."

And then, in his joy, he recited aloud from one of his psalms:

> *"My heart is not proud*
> *And my eyes are not lofty."*

He strolled back along the pond to the moss-covered rock. And then he said,

"O Lord of the world, is there any creature on earth that praises Thee and glorifies Thee as much as I do?"

With that, the frog went "Kerplunk" off the rock into the water! He began croaking loudly.

David stopped and looked down into the pond at the frog.

"Such noise," he said. "Why, O Frog, do you have to be so noisy?"

"Why indeed," the frog retorted, climbing out of the water again and perching himself on his stone.

"Indeed, King David," he said. "You are not as modest as first I thought. I just heard you boast that you praise the Lord more than any one else."

"Now in truth," David answered angrily. "Have I not written many psalms of praise?"

"But you are not the only one who praises the Lord," the frog said. "The earth praises Him, and the sun and the moon and every breathing thing. Didn't you just say in your last poem,

"*'Let every thing that hath breath praise the Lord.'*"

"True, true," the King said. "I did write those words."

"And they were words of truth," the frog said. "The whole world sings to the God of the Universe. Why, *I* praise Him too."

"You!" King David laughed.

The frog croaked and said, "There's no reason for you to laugh at me, David, just because you are a King and I am a frog. Let me tell you this, David. You sing unto the Lord, but I, besides singing to Him, have used my very *body* in His service."

"What do you mean, your body?" David asked. "How could your body help the Creator of the world?"

"Just seat yourself, David, and I will tell you."

David re-seated himself on the silken cushions. The frog croaked once to clear his throat. Then he said,

"Many long years ago, when the people of Israel was still enslaved in Egypt by Pharoah, you remember that the Lord sent plagues to Egypt."

David nodded.

The frog continued. "One of the plagues He sent was the plague of frogs. Listen closely, O King. I was the first frog to appear in Egypt, and by my loud, strong croaking, I summoned all the other frogs to come and over-run the land. My brothers came from everywhere. And we sacrificed our bodies in Egypt, bursting through the hardest of bronze gates and marble walls to enter the palaces of Pharoah. Whenever I came to a palace built of marble, I called out:

"*'Make way that I may do the will of the Creator,'*

Immediately the marble would begin to crack. Yes, indeed, we performed great service for the Lord in Egypt. And ever since then I, the frog, remembering my past service, praise God and sing to Him day and night without stopping."

"All I hear from you," David said, "from early dawn till late at night, is your croaking."

"That croaking is my constant praise of the Lord."

"Then you were right to rebuke me," David said. "I am glad you did. I had become too proud. I began to think I was the only one who continually sang praises to Him."

"Everything does," the frog said. "But no one else is as fortunate as you, to have your songs written down for other people to sing. I know that generation after generation will talk of David, the Sweet Singer of Israel. They will sing your songs down through the ages."

"I thank you, friend Frog."

"David, King David," the frog said timidly. "May I ask a great favor? At dawn you have walked by this pond and I have heard you recite, 'The heavens declare the glory of God.' David, O King David, would you let *me* sing that song with you?"

"Certainly," said David, "now that I know that your voice is in praise of God."

So there sounded from David's garden a strange duet, the deep croaking of the frog and the clear voice of the Sweet Singer of Israel.

The Magic Crown

Early one morning King David sat on the terrace playing his harp. He was singing one of his songs:

> "The earth is the Lord's, and the fulness thereof;
> The world and they that dwell therein."

At that moment, a knock sounded on the door, and in strode Joab, the general of the King's armies.

"Greetings, Your Majesty," Joab said, and then burst out irritably. "This is no time to play the harp."

"Greetings, Joab," David the King answered. "It is always time to sing a song of praise."

"Oh, Your Majesty," said Joab impatiently. "The whole world conspires against you, and you sit here and sing songs!"

King David laughed. "Sit you down, Joab. Here, be seated."

He motioned towards a carved chair of stone. Joab strode to it and seated himself.

King David said, "You have rebuked me, Joab, and that rebuke makes me feel like a boy again. When I was a lad, living in my father's house, my brothers used to taunt me and call me 'the singer of songs.' Now I am an old, old King and the general of my own armies scolds me because I sit and sing my songs."

"I didn't mean to rebuke the King," Joab said gruffly.

"Yes, you did," David said. "But I forgive you. As for being in danger, all my life I have been in danger. I fought the wild beasts of the forests to protect my flocks. I spent many years fleeing the wrath of King Saul in his madness. The Philistines warred against me, and the Jebusites. And Shobach and his Arameans I defeated. Now I am an old man. Surely I have earned the right to sing my songs in peace. All my enemies have been conquered."

"Not all your enemies!" Joab exclaimed.

"Yes, all my enemies," King David insisted. "There is no one who wishes me harm."

"O David, O King David." Joab turned to plead with him. "Listen to me. I am your old friend. Side by side we conquered the Philistines and the Jebusites. But now there is an enemy within our line and within your household."

"Oh, my old comrade," David said. "You are always seeing danger."

"No, listen to me, David," pleaded Joab. "You are getting old. One day, perhaps soon, perhaps far off, I do not know when, but one day death will come to you as it comes to all men."

"Then I will go the way of all flesh," the King said. "I am prepared to meet death, Joab."

"You are not prepared to meet death," Joab said sternly. "Not until you have settled one question: — Who is to be the King after you?"

The King put down his harp and stared at Joab. "Who is to be King after me? Why, one of my sons, of course!"

"Of course," Joab nodded. "But which one?"

"Which one?" David said. "I have not given it a thought."

"You have not, O King," Joab answered. "But your sons have. In fact, one of them, your son Absalom, cannot wait for the time of your death. He is already planning a rebellion against you."

"Absalom, my son? My son Absalom?" David said, bewildered.

"Absalom, your son," Joab said firmly. "He will, if he can, wrest your kingdom away from you. As for Adonijah, your son, he does not even bother to rebel. He is already thinking of himself as King. He has hired fifty men who run before him, shouting, 'Make way for the King of Israel'."

"Adonijah?" King David said, frowning.

"Yes, and even Chileab," Joab said quietly. "Chileab, it is true, is a great scholar. But even he, with his head dug into his books all the time, even Chileab is wondering if perhaps it should be he who should reign after you."

"And Amnon?" King David asked. "What of my son Amon?"

"Amnon." Joab said the name with scorn. "Amnon would wish to be King, of course. But Amnon spends his days drinking and carousing, and his nights he spends carousing and drinking. Yet Amnon would be King if he could."

"And young Solomon?" King David looked at Joab.

"Young Solomon," Joab said quietly, "is too young perhaps to know that he too could be King. But his mother . . . ah yes, Bathsheba plans that some day Solomon shall be King of Israel."

"So all my sons wish to be King after me?" David said. "Well, we shall see. Joab, my friend, go. Call my sons. Call Absalom, call Adonijah and Chileab, yes even Amnon. Call Solomon. Tell my sons to present themselves in the Throne Room within the hour."

Joab turned towards the door. The King called him back.

"And Joab," he said. "Call the Sanhedrin, the high court of Israel. Summon Ira and Mephibosheth, the learned scholars. Summon the great lawyers of the courts. Call them all together."

King David rose from his chair and walked into his bedchamber. He went directly to the ebony chest on which his crown lay. Joab hurried before him, to help the King. He reached over to pick up the crown to hand it to him. King David watched him, smiling.

Now Joab was a strong man, but when he went to pick up the crown, he found that he couldn't lift it. He couldn't budge it. He tried again and still he couldn't move it. He frowned, and tried a third time.

King David nudged Joab gently to one side. Joab looked at the King who, now that he was old, was thin and frail looking. And Joab thought, if I cannot lift that heavy crown, then surely the King, who is so much weaker than I, will not be able to.

But King David put his hands around the crown, lifted it easily from the chest and raised it up and put it on his head. Joab stared at him, astonished.

He said, "David, you have always entered the audience chamber with your crown on your head. I never knew that there was a miracle in the act of lifting it."

King David smiled at him and said, "Go, Joab. Go and summon my sons.

Go and summon the wise men of the kingdom."

One hour later, King David was in the audience chamber seated on his throne. In front of him, in a semicircle, sat his sons, Absalom, Adonijah, Chileab, Amnon and young Solomon. Behind them, in a semicircle, sat Ira and Mephibosheth, King David's teachers, and the learned scholars. And behind them in a semicircle sat the tribunal of lawyers, the wisest of men who belonged to the Sanhedrin, the highest court in the land.

At King David's right, Joab the warrior stood guard. At the King's left rested his Bell of Justice, and his harp. As quiet descended on the assembly, the King spoke.

"As King of Israel I have ruled for many, many years. And now I am become old. Soon another King will rule Israel.

"Nay, speak not thus," murmured Ira.

"Put not such thoughts into words," said Mephibosheth.

But King David nodded. "I shall go the way of all flesh, and a new King shall rule in Israel, and, according to God's promise, he shall be of my house. Now here before me are seated the wisest lawyers of the land and the scholars, all the teachers who have studied the law. And also before me are seated my sons, Absalom and Adonijah, Chileab and Amnon and Solomon. And from amongst my sons will come the future King of Israel."

Absalom sat in rigid silence. Adonijah stared straight ahead. Chileab looked down at the floor under his feet. And Amnon smiled to himself, not even listening to the King, thinking of the party he had attended the evening before. But young Solomon watched his father closely and listened to every word.

"Today," the King continued, "we shall select the future King of Israel."

Now Absalom arose. "My father, permit me to say a word."

King David nodded.

Absalom turned to face the scholars and the lawyers. He frowned slightly as he spoke.

"I am my father's eldest son. As the eldest son, the Crown of David must

rightfully come to me. I see no reason for this session of the court and the school to select a future King. *I* am the future King of Israel!"

"And I say I am!" Adonijah jumped to his feet and stood beside his brother.

"My sons," David said quietly. "Resume your seats."

He waited while they did, though Absalom scowled and Adonijah frowned. Then King David spoke again.

"There are certain tests, my sons, which will decide who is to be the future King of Israel. The one amongst you who shall be able to answer certain questions, he shall be King of Israel."

"Very well, then," Absalom said loudly. "Ask these questions."

King David turned to Joab and handed him a parchment on which there was writing in gold letters.

Joab held the parchment scroll in front of him and read the first question in a loud voice:—

"What is everything? What is nothing?"

King David said, "Absalom, you may answer."

Absalom glared at his father, then turned his head away.

King David said, "Adonijah, would you answer?"

Adonijah frowned at Joab, then stared at the parchment as if to look through it for the answer.

"Chileab?" King David said. "You are a great scholar. Answer the question."

"I'm sorry, my father," said Chileab. "I cannot."

"It may be," King David said, "that Amnon knows the answer?"

But Amnon wasn't even listening.

And King David turned to young Solomon. "I shall repeat the question, Solomon, my son. 'What is everything? What is nothing?' Perhaps you know the answer."

"Yes, my father," Solomon said quietly. "The world is nothing. God is everything."

David the King smiled. "My son Solomon has passed the first test which the future King of Israel is required to pass. Now we shall go on to the second."

"I protest!" Absalom cried, jumping to his feet.

"And I protest!" shouted Adonijah jumping to his feet.

"I object!" cried Ira.

"And I object!" cried Mephibosheth.

King David picked up the Bell of Justice and it rang loud and clear, sounding out over the protesting voices until they fell silent. King David said,

"Ira, speak your protest."

Ira rose and said loudly, "It is true that young Solomon passed the first test. He has answered the question which your other sons could not answer. But suppose, Your Majesty, that he wins out also in the second test? Surely your Highness does not presume to suggest that a mere lad of fourteen would become the King of Israel?"

King David nodded. "If Solomon will pass the second test, he shall surely be named my successor."

Mephibosheth rose to his feet. "But he is a mere lad, Your Majesty. He cannot have the knowledge and the experience for so great a responsibility."

"You have my permission," the King said, leaning back in his throne, "to ask young Solomon any question which you, or any scholar, or any member of the Sanhedrin thinks wise to ask. If young Solomon fails to answer one single question, then we shall say that he has not the knowledge or the experience to rule over Israel."

Thereupon, for the next hour, all the scholars gathered around Solomon. They asked him questions of science and medicine. They tested his knowledge of phil-

osophy. They questioned him on matters of religion. They fired questions at him, in rapid succession. But every question which was put to him, he answered without hesitation. Sometimes he even had the answer ready before the question was really asked.

At the end of the hour the scholars retired, defeated. Solomon had not failed in a single test.

Then the Sanhedrin gathered around Solomon. They asked him questions of law and ethics. They queried him on matters concerning truth and justice. Every lawyer asked him a difficult question, questions which some of the lawyers themselves could not answer. But Solomon knew exactly what to reply to each one. They kept at him for an hour, asking question after question, and each one Solomon answered as quickly as if he himself had written the law books.

And at the end of the hour, the lawyers retired, defeated. Solomon had succeeded in answering every single question.

"Your Majesty," Ira said, bowing to the King. "The lad has answered every question put by the scholars."

"Your Highness," said the head of the Sanhedrin, bowing to the King. "Young Solomon has answered every question put to him by the Sanhedrin."

King David smiled. "Then," he said, "we are ready for the second part of the test. All of you present can see the crown which I wear upon my head."

Every person in the room looked at the King's crown, but none more longingly than Absalom and Adonijah.

"This crown," said David, "is a magic crown. When first it was made for me, it was so heavy that no person in the world could lift it. Whereupon I had inscribed upon it the Name of the Lord. After that I, David, the King of Israel, have been able to lift this crown and set it upon my head. Only that man who will rule as King after me will have the strength to lift this crown from my head and place it upon his own."

Absalom looked at the crown and thought, why, it's made only of gold. I shall be able to lift it off my father's head and set it on my own.

Adonijah looked at the crown and thought, why, those sapphires and emeralds do not add to its weight. I shall be able to lift it easily enough.

Chileab and Amnon looked at the crown and Chileab thought, it will be too heavy for me. And Amnon thought, why, it's big enough to hold at least a quart of wine.

Young Solomon looked at the crown and thought, I wonder if I shall be able to lift it? I answered the questions, but I wonder if I'm worthy enough to take the crown from David's head!

"Absalom," King David ordered. "Come forward. Lift the crown from my head to yours."

Absalom strode forward eagerly and reached out his hands and grasped the crown. But, pull as he would, tug as he did, the crown remained firmly on David's head.

"Adonijah," David commanded. "Come forward. Lift the crown from my head to yours."

Adonijah rushed forward, smiling, and pushed at the crown even before he grasped it. But pull and thrust as he would, he could not dislodge the crown. It remained firmly set on the King's head.

Then Chileab tried, but he could not lift it off. And even Amnon paid attention long enough to know that he was to try to lift his father's crown off his head. But he couldn't budge it.

"Solomon!" David ordered. "You may come forward. Solomon, my son, you may try to lift the crown off the head of the King."

Solomon walked to the throne. He bowed to his father. Then he lifted his hands up to the King's head. And everyone in the throne room held his breath.

Solomon put his hands around the crown. With the tips of his fingers, he lifted it off as easily as if it were made of feathers. He set it on his own head.

A cheer broke out from the lawyers and the scholars. Only the other sons were silent.

Then King David said, "Here before you stands the future King of Israel. Solomon, my son, answered the questions which were asked of him. Solomon, my son, lifted the magic crown from off my head and placed it on his own. Because his wisdom in answering was confirmed by the magic crown, Solomon, my son, will be King of Israel!"

The Guard of Eagles

At the creation of the world, Adam had made a contract. He had promised the Most High to give to David a gift of *seventy* years of his own life. Adam had made that gift and David had now lived through those seventy years. Now the time had come when the terms of Adam's contract had been fulfilled. Now the time had come when David must die.

One morning, just before that sad event was to occur, David awoke from a dream just as young Solomon came into his bedchamber.

"You look ill, father," Solomon said. "What's wrong?"

"Oh, I've had a frightening dream," the King answered. "I dreamed that I would die on one of the Sabbaths in this, my seventieth year. It was God Himself Who spoke to me and told me this."

"That you would die!" Solomon exclaimed. "Oh, but it was only a dream, thank God for that. It was only a dream."

"But in that dream, *God* appeared to me," King David said, "and thus I know it to be a real warning. So I must set my house in order and prepare to die."

"But isn't there any way you could ward off death?" Solomon pleaded.

"Ward it off?" David asked doubtfully. "Let me think. Yes, there is! There is a way! It has been told me that I shall die on a Sabbath. But hear me, my son. The Angel of Death has no power to take the life of a man while he is studying the Torah. Therefore, my son Solomon, every Sabbath day I shall study the Torah so long and so constantly, that the Angel of Death will never be able to reach me!"

"A wonderful solution!" Solomon cried. "You are the first man in the world to have thought of a way to outwit the Angel of Death."

"Not the first," David said, shaking his head. "Have I never told you how Moses tried to escape death?"

Solomon frowned, puzzled. "No father, you never told me that story."

"I shall tell you now," David said. "Moses wished to hold off the hour of his death as long as possible. Knowing that the Angel of Death could not take a man's soul while he is studying the Torah, Moses engaged himself in the task of writing out thirteen Scrolls of the Law. He made one for each of the twelve tribes and one for the Holy Ark. These Scrolls were so perfect that the Angel Gabriel asked to have one of them fetched to him in heaven and he went about to all the seven heavens showing this Torah which Moses had written, to show what a wonderful scholar and scribe Moses had been."

"Yes, yes, go on," Solomon said eagerly.

"But, of course," David sighed. "It did not help. When the time came for Moses to die, he died, as every man born on earth must die. Every man must accept it and without anger or sadness, my son, not if he has lived a good and useful life."

"As you have, my father," Solomon said.

"I hope my life has been useful," David said. "So I shall try not to be sad at my approaching end. Still, I shall ward off the Angel of Death as long as I can. Every Sabbath I shall study the Torah without stop."

And so he did.

Before sundown on Fridays, before the beginning of the Sabbath, King David went into his study, took the Torah down from the shelf, placed it on his desk, ready to start studying the moment dusk fell. And to be sure that he did not misjudge the time, he actually began to study a half hour early, so that when the sun went down on Friday nights and the first stars began to shine, heralding the coming of a new Sabbath, David was hard at work, reading the Torah.

He read all night long, not stopping for a moment. He read in the morning, every second of it. All the long Saturday afternoons found him reading and studying the Law. And even when the sun went down in the late afternoons on Saturday, and the first stars began to shine to proclaim that the Sabbath had ended, still David studied for an extra half hour to be absolutely sure that the Sabbath was over.

In this way he outwitted the Angel of Death Saturday after Saturday.

Each Friday at sundown, the Angel of Death, invisible because of his magic black wings, flew down to the garden of David the King, in Jerusalem. And there he waited, trying to catch the King at a moment when he was not studying, so that he could take his soul up to heaven. But each Sabbath he failed, because David was so occupied in studying the Torah.

Each week, the Angel of Death began to arrive earlier and earlier, hoping that one Sabbath he would be able to reach the King before he could get to his desk and begin his studies. But, no matter how early the Angel of Death came, the King was already engaged in study. If he came at six o'clock, he was a half hour too late. If he came at five-thirty, he was fifteen minutes too late. If he came at five o'clock, he was five minutes too late.

And so it went, week after week. In the garden of the King, the Angel of Death sat baffled. After several weeks had passed, he began to lose patience. He had so much work to do, and here he was spending all this time trying to get this one soul into heaven.

One week he sat in the royal apple orchard hoping the King would forget and come strolling beside his favorite pond, to talk to the frog who lived there. One week the Angel of Death sat in the royal rose garden, knowing that the King liked the fragrance of the flowers, hoping he would come to enjoy the sight and scent of the roses. One week the Angel of Death hovered near the water gardens. It was a warm evening. Perhaps the King would come out for a breath of air, to sit beside the fountain and dip his hands into the rippling water to cool them off.

But on Sabbaths the King never stirred from his desk. He studied the Torah, Saturday after Saturday.

Now one Sabbath, the Angel of Death, weary of waiting, winged his way right to the window of the study. He whispered into the room, trying to make his voice sound like young Solomon's.

"Father, come out to the rose garden."

King David knew at once who it was and said, "Get thee gone, unwelcome one." And he never raised his eyes from the Torah.

The next week, the Angel of Death hovered near the garden door leading out of the King's study, and said in a voice which sounded like Abigail's, the King's wife,

"Dear husband, come out into the garden with me."

But again he did not fool the King who shouted, "Get thee gone, unwelcome one." And he never raised his eyes from the Torah.

On the next Friday eve, late at night, the Angel of Death sat on the terrace, wrapped in invisibility, wondering glumly when he would ever get this one task completed.

Up in his study, the King was studying the Torah.

Suddenly there was a loud brassy noise from the terrace, sounding through the night. It sounded as if some musicians had dropped a dozen cymbals.

The King, without lifting his eyes from the Torah, raised his voice and called to his daughter,

"Tamur, go to the terrace and see what that noise is."

Tamur went down the stairs leading from the King's study to the terrace. But when she got there she saw no one and heard nothing. She came back up the stairs.

"I heard no noise, father, and the terrace is empty."

"Very well, Tamur. Thank you."

Tamur left him alone and David continued his study. All at once the banging, clanging noise broke out again.

"Solomon!" King David called without raising his eyes from his book. "Solomon, my son, go see, please, what that clatter is out on the terrace."

"Certainly, father, I will," Solomon said. "Just you keep on studying the Torah, dear father."

"That I shall," David said, without interrupting his work for one second.

The banging and the clattering continued out on the terrace. But Solomon, going swiftly down the stairs, did not hear the noise. When he reached the terrace, he looked and saw no one. The terrace seemed to be empty. He searched all around, under the stone chairs, under the iron table, even in the potted plants at the stairway.

Then he came back into his father's study.

"Father," he said, "there is no one on the terrace. And father, I did not even hear any noise."

"Very well," David said. "Thank you, my son. And forgive me for disturbing your sleep."

"I gladly serve you, dear father," Solomon said. "Just you keep on studying."

And so the hours passed, quickly for those who were sleeping that night, slowly for David who was getting very tired and very weary as each hour passed. But soon the first streaks of light began to break up the night sky. The roosters in

the barnyards began to crow, welcoming a new dawn, urging the sleepy heads to get out of bed: "Another day is here, get out of bed, get out of bed!"

King David heard the crowing of the cocks and knew that the dawn had come. But weary as he was, there was no sleep for him. He still had the whole morning and the whole afternoon in which he must study constantly.

And now, down on the terrace, suddenly, with a great clanging and crashing and clattering, the noise which had disturbed him all night broke out anew.

"That noise makes me very nervous," David said, jumping up from his desk.

He forgot that he must not leave the Torah!

It was the Sabbath! And David was not studying the Torah! He strode quickly towards the stairway. And the Angel of Death was quick to seize his opportunity. David started down the stairs to see what all the commotion was about. He slipped. He lost his footing. He fell down the length of the stairs.

And thus King David died.

At that moment young Solomon came into his father's study with a cup of hot broth. He saw that his father's chair was empty.

"Father!" he cried, dropping the cup of soup. "Father, father, where are you?"

He rushed down the stairs, and then near the bottom, he went more slowly as he saw his father lying at the foot of the stairs on the terrace with the sun streaming down on him. The household was aroused and in the midst of everyone's grief at losing their father and their King, there was one more grief.

This was the Sabbath day and they could not move the King's body. But it was cruel to leave him lying in the sun until the Sabbath should end. What could they do?

While they stood there pondering the question, worrying and grieving, a whirring noise sounded in the air. A dark cloud seemed to float across the sun. Everyone looked up to see a giant eagle winging his way towards the terrace.

And as they watched, the eagle swooped down until he was about ten feet above the body of the King. There he stayed, suspended in air, his huge wings spread out. A moment later another eagle joined him, hovering the same distance above the King, and he too spread out his wings, covering and shielding the King from the sun. And then came a third eagle, a large, white eagle, and he hovered in the air, protecting King David's body from the glare of the sun.

And throughout the whole of that Sabbath day, this Guard of Eagles shielded the King of Israel. When the day ended and sun sank in the west and the white moon came out with her soft, glowing light, Solomon picked up his father's body to carry it up to his bed.

With a flap of their wings, the King's Guard of Eagles swooped up into the sky and flew away.

The Pasha's Dagger

After King David's death, his son Solomon built a magnificent tomb for him. It was made of marble and granite, with many windows of different colors. And it contained a series of marble staircases descending downward into the earth.

Into this tomb, Solomon placed many treasures of silver and gold, of diamonds and rubies.

This tomb of many windows contained only one door, a heavy door made of bronze with iron hinges. This door was always kept locked, its key in the possession of the Keeper of the Door.

Many people came to see the Tomb of David. They came from far and near, from the neighboring countries and from the deserts. Some came to see the last resting-place of the King they had loved so well. Some came out of curiosity because the news of this magnificent tomb had spread to every corner of the world. And some came in the hope of getting into the tomb and making off with some of the treasures hidden there.

One day, many centuries after the death of David, a Moslem Pasha came from India to Jerusalem on a visit. He was a rich man and he came accompanied by a large following of servants and friends. At first the Pasha pretended to be interested in visiting the whole city. On the first day he went on an inspection tour of the palaces and then of the schools. On the second day, he went to the market-place and to the Temple mount.

But on the third day, he finally approached the real object of his visit. He and his company went to see David's Tomb as if it were just one of the many sights of interest.

Arriving at the heavy bronze door, the Pasha strode directly up to the Keeper of the Door. He made a sign of greeting, and said,

"I desire entrance to the Tomb."

The Keeper of the Door said, "I regret that cannot be, sir. No one is permitted entrance to the Tomb."

"But I have come all the way from India to see this Tomb!" the Pasha insisted.

The Keeper of the Door merely shrugged. "I am sorry, Your Excellency. No one is admitted to the Tomb."

The Pasha turned away, a scowl puckering his forehead. One of his captains plucked at his sleeve, pulled him out of the guard's hearing, and then whispered,

"Your Highness, I have discovered an open window which could lead one down into the Tomb. We could lower one of the men deep down into the Tomb, and he could fill a sack with jewels . . ."

The Pasha interrupted him. "Show me this window."

"Here it is, Your Majesty."

The Captain led him around the corner until they came to a window made of ruby-colored glass. It was only half open, but enough to allow a small man to crawl through.

The Pasha stood at the window pretending to be studying the glass. Tucked into the sash at his waist, he wore a valuable little dagger with a pearl and diamond handle. As if absent-mindedly, absorbed in thinking of something, he took the dagger out of his sash, leaned against the window, trying to peer down into the Tomb. He was idly playing with the dagger, tossing it from one hand to the other.

Then suddenly, he dropped the weapon! And it fell, down, down into the Tomb of David.

"My dagger!" the Pasha cried. "My pearl and diamond dagger! It has fallen into the tomb."

"How dreadful!" exclaimed the scheming captain. "How shall we get it back?"

The Pasha pretended to think deeply. Then he turned to his company and said,

"I have lost my valuable dagger which was given to me by my father's father.

There is only one way to retrieve it. Someone must be lowered through the window and find my treasure. Who will go for me?"

"I shall go." A small, thin man stepped forward.

"Good," the Pasha said. "You are a faithful servant and I shall reward you."

He led the small thin man up to the window, and then whispered,

"In that tomb there are many, many treasures. Take this blue velvet sack. Bring up as many treasures as you can carry in this sack, and half shall be your reward."

The man's eyes sparkled with greed. He whispered,

"Hurry and lower me, sir. I shall bring up many jewels."

The captain brought a stout rope which he tied around the man's waist. He held the loose end of the rope and the man climbed up to the window sill, and then slowly, the captain began to lower the man into the Tomb. After a few moments, the captain said,

"I believe he must have reached the bottom because the rope is not pulling out any more. He will soon give us the signal to pull him up."

After a few minutes, the captain said,

"Your Highness, I believe there is something wrong. Surely the man would have filled that small sack with jewels by now. Why does he not give me a signal to pull him up?"

"Signal him," the Pasha ordered.

The captain jerked on the rope. Nothing happened. He jerked again.

"I get no response," he said. "I fear something has gone wrong, Your Majesty."

"Pull him up," commanded the Pasha.

Another officer came forward and helped the captain. They pulled and pulled on the rope, and it was so heavy that a third officer came to help them. Then all three pulled together, and finally they pulled up the small, thin man, up from the tomb, up out of the window. But, as they brought him up to the windowsill, someone cried out.

"He is dead!"

It took only one look at the pasty whiteness of the little man's face for the Pasha to see that indeed he was dead.

The officers brought the man down off the windowsill, untied the rope, and moved him over to one side. The Pasha turned to his men again and said,

"Who will now go down and find my dagger?"

This time a tall man stepped forward. He too was quite thin.

"Let me try," he said. "I will get the Pasha's dagger."

They tied the rope around his waist, and the Pasha whispered to him,

"Down there you will find many, many treasures. Bring as many as you can carry in this red velvet sack, and I shall give you half."

The man grasped the red velvet sack, and said, "I shall bring you many treasures."

As he stepped up to the windowsill, the captain said,

"When you get to the bottom, give the rope a little jerk, so that I shall know you are down."

The tall, thin man waved the blue velvet sack, smiled, and then his head slid out of view as the captain began to lower the rope. The rope went sliding through his hands faster and faster. And then it stopped. But the signal he was waiting for did not come.

"Now why doesn't he jerk the rope!" he exclaimed. "He just hangs there like a dead weight."

"Again?" one of the officers asked. "Another dead weight? Perhaps he too is dead."

"Nonsense," declared the Pasha. "Why should he be dead too? That first man was a weakling and would have died anyway."

"But the rope remains heavy in my hands," complained the captain.

"Very well, pull him up," growled the Pasha.

Again it took three men to pull up the man on the rope. And again as his face came into view, one of the men in the crowd shouted,

"Look! He is dead too!"

And he was, just as dead as the first man.

The Pasha's company began to edge backward, away from the two dead men, away from the Pasha and the officers, away from the Tomb of David. The captain untied the rope from the dead man's waist, and rolled him on the ground next to the first man.

The Pasha turned to his company with a smile.

"Come, come," he said, smiling broadly, speaking slowly. "Is there no one brave enough to volunteer to go down into the tomb for me? There is nothing to hurt you down there. These two men were sickly men. That's why they died. Give me a strong man. Give me a courageous man who will go down and get the dagger of my father's father. To him I will give a great reward."

But the men kept pushing backward.

The Pasha smiled again and said coaxingly, "Would you have me think that you are a pack of cowards? Would you have me go down into the tomb myself to find the dagger? Would you? Speak up! Is there a brave man amongst you or shall I go myself?"

One tall, broad, strong man separated himself from the group and strode forward.

"I shall go, Your Highness."

"Ah, a brave man!" The Pasha smiled. "To him shall I give double the reward I promised the others." Then he whispered to the man, "Take this green velvet sack. In the tomb you will find many treasures, many precious jewels. Rubies and diamonds and pearls are there in great abundance. Bring me as many as you can get into this sack, and I shall give you half."

The tall, broad, strong man smiled in satisfaction, grasped the green velvet sack, strode to the window and waited impatiently while the captain tied the rope around his waist.

"Hurry, O captain, hurry," he said, thinking how rich he soon would be.

The captain began to lower him down the window, but he was so heavy that the other two officers had to help. They gave out the rope slowly so that it would not burn their hands. And slowly they lowered the man down into the tomb. This time they felt his feet bump against the earth and felt a jerk on the rope which told them he was down. But they clung tightly to the rope, waiting for the second signal which would tell them to pull up.

They waited and waited. And no signal came. Finally, when many minutes had passed, the captain said,

"I wonder why he does not signal."

"Give him a few more minutes," the Pasha said, thinking that the man was taking so long because he had to stuff so many jewels into the green velvet sack.

But when another ten minutes went by, the men began to murmur. Someone in the crowd shouted,

"I'll wager he's dead too."

"Pull him up," the Pasha whispered to the captain, not liking the angry murmuring of the crowd of men behind him.

The three officers began to pull and pull, but the rope was so heavy that this time, three more men had to come and help. And they pulled and pulled, and up they pulled the tall and broad and strong man. He too was dead. No one shouted it aloud this time. They just moved back and back, away from the three dead men lying at the feet of the Pasha.

Now the Pasha roared in anger. "They steal my dagger! They kill my men! Revenge! I shall have revenge for this!"

Leaving a guard over the bodies of the three dead men, the Pasha, followed by his worried officers and his grumbling company, strode through the streets of Jerusalem until he came to the house of the Hakam Bashi, the chief Rabbi. In a few moments the Hakam Bashi came out and greeted the Pasha who did not respond to the greeting at all. Instead he ordered,

"Send one of your men into the Tomb of David."

"The Tomb of David?" the Hakam Bashi asked quietly. "I regret, sir, that no one is ever permitted to enter the Tomb."

"I do not care what is permitted," the Pasha said. "I have dropped a most valuable weapon into the tomb. I tried to recover it myself by lowering my men into the tomb. But each man I sent died there. I warn you, Hakam Bashi. If my weapon is not restored to me before night falls, I shall destroy your synagogues!"

With that, he turned on his heel and strode away.

The Hakam Bashi rushed back into the house, and sent messengers for all the chief men of the city to come quickly. When they had gathered, he said,

"The Pasha has dropped his dagger into the Tomb of David. He demands its return. If we do not restore it to him, he will destroy our synagogues."

One scholar spoke up, "But it will be impossible to find the weapon. It is forbidden for any person to enter the Tomb."

"Three of the Pasha's men have already died in the Tomb." Spoke up another man. "If we send any one into the Tomb, we shall be sending that man to his death."

"This is a tragic choice," said a scribe. "It is the welfare of our community against the life of one man. But we must make that choice. We must send one man."

"But who will volunteer?" the Hakam Bashi said. "We cannot force any one person to risk his life."

"We must cast lots," said the scholar who had spoken first.

Everyone agreed that casting lots would be the fairest way. The Hakam Bashi arranged long strips of parchment, as many as there were men in the room. All the strips were blank except one and on that one the Kakam Bashi wrote the Name of God.

"Now," he said, placing the parchment strips into an ivory box and shaking it up well. "We will each select a strip of parchment. Whoever selects the strip of parchment on which I have writen the Name of God, that person will go into the Tomb and retrieve the Pasha's dagger."

A slight shiver ran through the men. They began to move forward to select their parchment strips. The first man drew out the first strip.

"Blank!" someone shouted. "You are lucky!"

The next man put in his hand and out came a parchment strip which had no writing on either side.

"Lucky!" someone yelled at him. "You stay safely at home."

And so into the ivory box, man after man put in his hand and pulled out a blank parchment strip.

Then up to the box stepped a young man whose name was Joel. He smiled as he put his hand into the ivory box. He lifted out a strip of parchment. He held it high for everyone to see.

"It is Joel on whom the lot has fallen!" someone cried.

"Joel has the strip with the Name of the Lord."

Joel held the strip of parchment in his hand and without saying anything to anyone, he turned to leave the room. At the door he looked back and said,

"Don't worry, friends. I'll see you soon. As soon as I've returned the jewelled dagger to the Pasha."

"May God protect you," his friends cried.

"Come back safely, Joel, come back safely."

As he started out the door, two of his friends came hurrying after him.

"We will go with you," one of them said.

"As far as the door of the Tomb," the other said.

The three men strode away from the Hakam Bashi's house, down the long and broad avenue, until they came to the Tomb of David. They walked up to the bronze door and Joel said to the Keeper of the Door,

"I am sent by the Hakam Bashi to go into the Tomb and retrieve the dagger of the Pasha."

The Keeper of the Door shook his head sadly. From the iron chain at his waist he lifted the huge key which unlocked the heavy bronze door. The key moved in the lock, and the Keeper turned the knob of the door and began to pull at it. With a great creaking and groaning, the heavy bronze door opened slowly.

"I shall see you soon," Joel cried to his friends.

"Hurry back, Joel."

And then Joel was inside the Tomb of David!

At the very top step of the marble staircase he stopped, and held his breath. Here he was, where he had often longed to be! Perhaps it meant death. Perhaps not. But it was exciting to be here, inside David's Tomb, where thousands of people had wanted to come and no one before him had dared to go.

Then, letting out the breath he had been holding, he started to go down the staircase. And with each step he took, the light became clearer and brighter. He walked down and down the marble staircase, and then as he began to get near the bottom, the light changed into pure white.

It was so white and so shining, it dazzled him, and for a moment he stood hesitating, not sure which way to turn to search for the dagger. As he stood there, suddenly he felt a slight stir in the air towards his left.

He turned his head and saw a very tall man coming towards him. This man was dressed all in white, from his white sandals to his white robe to the long, flowing white beard on his chin and the long, flowing white hair on his head. And through Joel's mind flashed the thought, "It is the Prophet Elijah come to help me!" Joel stood open-mouthed, staring at the noble figure which approached him.

Without saying a word, the man in white handed the pearl and diamond dagger and the three empty velvet sacks to Joel. Then the old man walked away from him very fast, so fast that in a moment he had disappeared into the white blinding light.

"Thank you, noble sir," Joel called through the light. "Thank you very much."

He turned and ran up the marble staircase until he reached the heavy bronze door. Out of the door he hurried and into the sunshine. His friends cheered him as he came out.

The men hurried back to the house of the Hakam Bashi where Joel turned over to the Hakam Bashi the Pasha's dagger and velvet sacks. These were given to the Pasha who left at once for India.

But the treasures which Solomon had placed into the Tomb of King David, remained there and are forever safe.